THE SUPER EASY MEDITERRANEAN DIET COOKBOOK FOR BEGINNERS ON A BUDGET:

250 5-ingredient Recipes that Anyone Can Cook Reset your Body and Boost your Energy
2-Week Mediterranean Diet Plan

By

DR. BELINDA MACK

TABLE OF CONTENTS

CHAPTER 10: 79

SNACKS 79

CHAPTER 11: 84

DESSERTS & FRUIT 84

INTRODUCTION

The Mediterranean diet varies from that of other diets as it builds on traditional nutritional regimes which people used to eat in countries such as Italy and Greece. Many scientists have found that the traditional Mediterranean menu is one of the most nutritious and healthiest in the world—ideal for weight reduction and lower rates of cardiovascular illnesses and other chronic conditions. The Mediterranean people have enjoyed the advantages of Mediterranean foods by way of following recipes that will delight your palate and nourish your body and soul. All can easily be prepared in your home kitchen.

Research has shown that the Mediterranean people are particularly healthy compared to people in the United States and had a low occurrence of many lifestyle illnesses.

Several studies have now shown that the Mediterranean diet can cause weight reduction and help prevent heart attacks, strokes, type 2 diabetes and premature death.

The Mediterranean diet has been recognized as an exceptionally healthy diet for longer life expectancy. Researchers have recognized the menu of vegetables, fruit, nuts, legumes, beans, olive oil and seafood and low intake of chicken, eggs and red meat as the most appropriate way to prevent chronic illnesses—particularly coronary heart diseases. It is the availability and right combination of these foods that make the Mediterranean diet healthy and balanced.

Many Americans and Europeans are affected by coronary heart illnesses, obesity, gallstones, diabetes and cancer caused by excessive intake of animal fats, inadequate diet and low exercise regimes. The Mediterranean diet matches set diet recommendations. It has become popular due to extensive studies and research performed on Mediterranean people.

This Mediterranean diet cookbook provides numerous techniques of food preparation such as appetizers, salads, desserts and main course meals. The people in the Mediterranean region practice these techniques. Most Mediterranean cookbooks fail to explain the everyday traditional Mediterranean diet and contain different variations of the recipes.

The recipes in this book are contemporary, new, and full of flavor combinations you may not have come across before.

What is the Mediterranean Diet?

The Mediterranean diet is a form of eating based on the old cuisine of the countries bordering the Mediterranean Sea. Although there is no single definition of the Mediterranean diet, it is usually rich in vegetables, fruits, whole grains, beans, nuts and seeds and olive oil.

The most important elements of the Mediterranean diet **include:**
- Daily consumption of vegetables, whole grains, fruits and healthy fats.
- Weekly consumption of fish, chicken, beans and eggs.
- Moderate portions of dairy products
- Limited consumption of red meat

Other essential Mediterranean Dietary Elements consist of enjoying a glass of fine, red wine while having one's meals in the company of one's family and friends as well as maintaining a physical and active lifestyle to keep in shape.

Plant-based

The Mediterranean diet is based on vegetables, fruits, herbs, nuts, beans, and whole grains. Meals are based on these plant foods. Moderate amounts of dairy products, poultry, and eggs are also essential for the Mediterranean diet, as is seafood. Red meat, on the other hand, is consumed only occasionally.

Healthy fat

Healthy fats are a pillar of the Mediterranean diet. They are consumed instead of saturated and trans fats, which contribute to heart disease.

Olive oil is the main source of added fats in the Mediterranean diet. Olive oil provides monounsaturated fatty acids that lower total cholesterol and low-density lipoprotein cholesterol (LDL or "bad" cholesterol). Nuts and seeds also contain monounsaturated fatty acids.

Another component essential to the Mediterranean diet is seafood, more specifically; fish such as mackerel, herring, sardines, albacore, salmon and many trout which are classified as oily fish and are abundant in omega-3 fatty acids. This is known to be a form of polyunsaturated fat that can help minimize body inflammation. Omega-3 fatty acids also help lower triglycerides, reduce blood clotting and reduce the risk of stroke and heart failure.

The Importance of Olive Oil

Almost all food researchers attribute at least some of the legendary health benefits of the Mediterranean diet to the abundant amounts of olive oil contained in nearly every meal. Olives are an ancient food, and olive trees have been growing around the Mediterranean region since around 3000 B.C.

Olive oil joins to foods containing omega-3 fatty acids, such as salmon and nuts, for example, as an elite class of healthy fatty acids. Olive oil has a lot of research that supports the health benefits; research shows that the FDA even allows labels on olive oil bottles containing a particular health claim (so far, this was only allowed for olive oil, omega-3 fatty acids, and nuts).

Why is olive oil so good for you?

Olive oil is rich in compounds called phenols, which are powerful antioxidants that can reduce inflammation and fight free radical damage. Olive oil consists mainly of monounsaturated fatty acids, the most important of which is oleic acid. It is known that oleic acid is extremely healthy for the heart in many ways, particularly compared to many other refined vegetable oils, trans-fatty acids, or hydrogenated fatty acids.

Olive oil even has a breakthrough in heart health benefits compared to most grain-based carbohydrates: some diets containing many monounsaturated fats reduce LDL cholesterol, increase HDL cholesterol and lower cholesterol HDL Triglycerides are better than rich carbohydrates diets, according to some studies.

How much olive oil do you need to consume daily?

Recommendations vary from one to four tablespoons depending on your caloric needs and your diet. Study shows that people in the Mediterranean probably consume between three and four tablespoons a day. This is the amount that some health professionals recommend for their patients with heart disease.

Remember that not all olive oil is made equal. Unfortunately, most commercial manufacturers provide all kinds of imitations and substandard products. The problem is that these oils are not always harvested or processed properly, which means that many of their delicate nutrients can be destroyed and some of their fatty acids can become toxic.

Look for labels indicating that your oil is "extra virgin" and ideally cold-pressed. Olive oil is rather unique among oils because it can be consumed in its raw form without any processing (you can press olives and enjoy their natural oils).

Although it's delicate and not necessarily the best cooking oil, cold-pressed or ejected oil is not refined; it retains all its natural vitamins, essential fatty acids, antioxidants and other nutrients.

Why the Mediterranean Diet?

Interest in the Mediterranean diet started in the 1960s with the observation that cardiovascular diseases have caused fewer deaths in Mediterranean regions such as Greece and Italy than in the United States and northern Europe. Subsequent studies have shown that the Mediterranean diet is associated with a reduction in risk factors for cardiovascular disease.

The Mediterranean diet is a healthy diet recommended by the USDA to promote health and prevent chronic diseases.

The World Health Organization also recognizes that it is a healthy and sustainable diet and an intangible cultural asset of the United Nations National Organization for Education, Science, and Culture.

Major Benefits of the Mediterranean Diet

The tradition and history of the Mediterranean diet come from the traditional food and social patterns of the regions of southern Italy, Greece, Turkey, and Spain. This is why the Mediterranean diet is not even a "diet", but rather a lifestyle. For thousands of years, the inhabitants of the Mediterranean coast have eaten a diet rich in fiber-diet of fruits and vegetables, proteins and fats in moderation, and a glass of locally made wine on occasion to complete a meal.

The Mediterranean diet has several advantages. Ingredients are now available and delicious dishes can be prepared quickly and easily.

Here are some of the most important benefits of the Mediterranean diet:

Low in processed foods and sugar

The diet consists of natural foods, including olive oil, legumes such as peas and beans, fruits and vegetables, unrefined grain products and small portions of animal products (always organic and locally produced). Unlike the standard American diet, it is low in sugar and essentially free of GMOs or artificial ingredients such as high fructose corn syrup, preservatives, and flavor enhancers. For something sweet, the Mediterranean people love fruit or small portions of homemade desserts with natural sweeteners such as honey.

In addition to plant foods, moderate consumption of locally caught fish and cow, goat, or sheep cheese and yogurt are other important components of the diet. Fish such as sardines and anchovies are a central part of the diet, which generally contains less meat than many Western diets.

Although most Mediterranean people are not vegetarians, the diet favors only low consumption of meat and heavier meals, opting for lighter and healthier fish options. This can be beneficial for people who want to lose weight and improve heart health, cholesterol and omega-3 fatty acid intake.

Assists healthy weight loss

If you want to lose weight without being hungry and maintain it in a realistic way throughout your life, this may be the answer. The diet is durable and valuable. It has been successfully used by many people around the world, especially because it helps to control weight and reduce fat consumption naturally and simply through the consumption of nutrient-rich foods.

The Mediterranean diet can be interpreted differently, whether you prefer to eat fewer carbohydrates, less protein, or somewhere in between. The diet focuses on the consumption of healthy fats, while carbohydrates are kept relatively low, and the consumption of foods high in high-quality protein is improved. If you prefer protein to legumes and cereals, you can lose weight in a healthy, non-deprived way, with a large amount of high-quality seafood and dairy products (which at the same time offer other benefits such as omega-3s and often probiotics).

Fish, dairy products and meat contain the healthy fatty acids that the body needs. They work to help you feel full, control your weight gain, regulate your blood sugar, your mood, and your energy level. But if you are more of a plant-based consumer, legumes and whole grains (especially if they are soaked and sprouted) are also good options.

Improves heart health

Research shows that greater compliance with the traditional Mediterranean diet, which includes monounsaturated and omega-3 fatty acids, is associated with a significant reduction in mortality, especially heart disease. Many studies have shown significant effects of a Mediterranean diet rich in alpha-linolenic acid (ALA) in olive oil. Some have discovered that a Mediterranean diet can reduce the risk of heart death by 30% and sudden cardiac death by 45%.

Olive oil is also beneficial for reducing hypertension because nitric oxide is more bioavailable, allowing it to dilate blood vessels and keep it clean. Another element of protection is that it helps to combat the effects of oxidation that promotes disease and improves endothelial function. People in the Mediterranean generally have no difficulty maintaining healthy cholesterol levels because they eat lots of healthy fats.

Helps fight cancer

A plant-based diet rich in fruits and vegetables is the cornerstone of the Mediterranean diet. It can help fight cancer, as it provides antioxidants, protects DNA from damage, stops cell mutation, reduces inflammation and slows tumor growth. Many studies indicate that olive oil can also be a natural treatment for cancer and can reduce the risk of colon cancer. It could have a protective effect on the development of cancer cells because it reduces inflammation and oxidative stress, while promoting a glycemic balance and healthy weight.

Prevents or treats diabetes

The Mediterranean diet is anti-inflammatory and may help fight diseases related to chronic inflammation, including metabolic syndrome and type 2 diabetes. It regulates excess insulin, a hormone that regulates the blood sugar level.

By regulating blood sugar with a balance of whole foods containing healthy fatty acids, high-quality protein sources and some low-sugar carbohydrates, the body burns fat more efficiently and has more energy. A low-sugar diet is part of a diet plan for natural diabetics.

The Mediterranean diet is low in sugar because the only sugar present comes mainly from fruits, wine, and sometimes local desserts. In terms of drinks, many people also drink lots of fresh water, coffee and red wine. Sodas and sugary drinks are not as popular in the Mediterranean as they are in the United States.

Although some Mediterranean diets contain a large number of carbohydrates, such as pasta and bread, being active and consuming minimal amounts of sugar means that insulin resistance is rare in these countries. The Mediterranean eating style helps to prevent peaks and troughs in the blood sugar level, which reduces energy and affects your mood. All of these different factors contribute to the diabetes prevention benefits of this diet.

Protects cognitive health and improves mood

Eating a Mediterranean diet can be a natural treatment for Parkinson's disease, a great way to protect your memory and a step in the right direction to treat Alzheimer's disease and dementia naturally. Cognitive impairment can occur when the brain does not receive enough dopamine, a chemical substance that is essential for the body to function properly.

It is known that healthy fats such as olive oil and nuts, as well as many anti-inflammatory fruits and vegetables, fight age-related cognitive impairment. This helps to counteract the harmful effects of exposure to toxicity, free radicals and poor diets that cause inflammation or food allergies, which can contribute to the deterioration of brain function. This is one of the reasons why respect for the Mediterranean diet is linked to lower rates for

Alzheimer's disease.

Probiotic foods such as yogurt and kefir also help to develop a healthy digestive system, which we now know are related to cognitive functions, memory and mood.

Increases longevity

A diet rich in fresh plant-based foods and healthy fats is a winning combination for long life. Monounsaturated fatty acids, found in olive oil and some nuts, are the main source of fat in the Mediterranean diet. Time and time again, studies have shown that monounsaturated fats are associated with low levels of heart disease, cancer, depression, cognitive diseases, Alzheimer's, inflammatory diseases, etc. Currently, heart disease is by far the leading cause of death in developed countries.

Relieves stress and promotes relaxation

Another important factor is that this diet encourages people to spend time in nature, to sleep well, and to work together to create healthy home cooked meals. All are great ways to relieve stress and, as a result, to prevent inflammation. In general, people living in these areas eat food surrounded by family and friends (rather than alone or on the road) and spend time laughing, dancing, gardening and enjoying life.

Chronic stress can affect your quality of life, your weight and your health. People who eat at a slow pace, consume natural, local foods and engage in regular physical activity are more likely to maintain a good mood.

The Mediterranean diet includes love and fascination for wine, especially red wine, which is considered moderately beneficial and protective. For example, red wine can help fight obesity. This smart choice for a healthy lifestyle leads to a longer life without chronic complications and stress-related illnesses, such as those caused by hormonal imbalances, fatigue, inflammation and weight gain.

Helps fight depression

According to a study, those who follow the Mediterranean diet can help reduce the risk of depression. Researchers participating in the study examined the mental health effects of adherence to various diets, such as the Mediterranean diet, the Healthy Eating Index (HEI) diet, Dietary approaches to stop hypertension (DASH diet), and the rate of inflammation of the diet. They found that the risk of depression decreased further when people followed a traditional Mediterranean diet and generally ate various anti-inflammatory foods.

Mediterranean Diet Meal Plan

It is easy to follow a Mediterranean diet plan because the food selection includes flavorful whole grains, fruits, vegetables, nuts, seeds, beans and fats. Perhaps the best advantage of following a Mediterranean diet meal plan is its effectiveness in losing dangerous belly fat.

Carrying extra weight can make a big difference in your general health chart. Too much belly fat leads to overcrowding of your internal organs, resulting in a chain reaction with adverse health effects: elevated levels of LDL cholesterol (hypertension), hypertension, diabetes and heart disease.

If you take a tape measure and wrap it around your abdomen at the level just above your hip bones and it is more than 40 centimeters if you are male or more than 35 centimeters, if you are female, you need a healthy change. The solution may be in your diet.

Details of the Mediterranean diet meal plan

I like to think of the Mediterranean diet meal plan with the food pyramid turned and brewed. Meaning the meal plan for the Mediterranean diet is less about meat and more about fruits, vegetables and whole grains and most importantly, the consumption of monounsaturated and polyunsaturated fats. Rather than a diet, this diet should be viewed as a different manner of eating along side a healthy way of life

Suhat of ch as Greece, Italy, France, Spain, and Morocco.

You can follow a Mediterranean diet or make your own meals from basic food. For example, you can start your day with fruit or an egg omelet with vegetables, snack on nuts, seeds and legumes, and a lunch and dinner party with salads, fish or white meat.

The food combinations on a Mediterranean meal plan are endless, making it an excellent diet for the creative chef.

Conclusion

Following a Mediterranean meal plan is a sure way to lose belly fat and fats from other parts of your body. The diet is naturally rich in fiber, vitamins, antioxidants and minerals, which means that your heart is protected while you lose weight.

Is your belly too big? Are you afraid that you have let your weight go too far and that you now feel worried about what you are going to do in the world to get rid of that belly fat?

I know how scary it can be, and I don't want you to follow a silly fat diet that promises fat loss very quickly, but ultimately makes you feel tired, angry and hungry.

Stop searching for fast solutions and get the solution.

What to Eat on the Mediterranean Diet Meal Plan

One of the benefits of the Mediterranean diet is the ease with which you can get the right foods and maintain good eating habits. Eating out at a restaurant can be a bit more difficult. In a world full of fast food, it takes some effort to maintain your Mediterranean diet. Here are some tips for finding or preparing Mediterranean diet meals when you are on-the-go.

Most of your diet should contain natural and unprocessed Mediterranean foods. This diet is not restrictive and allows you to enjoy delicious meals.

Mix in a wide range of foods to balance nutrients, vitamins and minerals. Whole foods (containing one ingredient) are essential to get the most out of your Mediterranean lifestyle.

Focus on food:

- **Produce:** eat lots of tomatoes, broccoli, spinach, kale, cauliflower, carrots, onions, Brussels sprouts, cucumbers, apples, bananas, pears, berries, oranges and melons.
- **Nuts and seeds:** eat at least a handful of almonds, walnuts, macadamia nuts, hazelnuts, cashews, sunflower seeds and pumpkin seeds.
- **Legumes:** eat more beans, peanuts, peas, lentils, chickpeas, etc. Legumes are an important source of fiber and protein on this diet.
- **Tubers:** potatoes, sweet potatoes, turnips, and yams are starchy vegetables to be consumed moderately.
- **Whole Grains:** consume small portions of whole oats, brown rice, rye, barley, corn, buckwheat, whole wheat and whole grains. Avoid refined carbohydrates.
- **Fish and other seafood:** eat salmon, sardines, trout, tuna, mackerel, shrimp, clams, crab, oysters or mussels at least twice a week.
- **Poultry:** occasionally, enjoy chicken, duck, turkey or other birds.
- **Eggs and dairy products:** cheese, yogurt and eggs are an excellent source of protein and healthy fats.
- **Herbs and spices:** accentuate your meals with garlic, basil, mint, rosemary, sage, nutmeg, cinnamon and pepper.
- **Healthy fats:** consume olive oil, nuts and avocado frequently.

Additionally, be sure to drink plenty of water, as well as a moderate amount of red wine, coffee, and tea. Remember that anyone with drinking problems should not consume wine, however.

What to Avoid while Following a Mediterranean Diet Meal Plan

If one looks at an Americanized dish, the majority of chefs supplement other well-established dishes from say, Italian cuisine, by adding extra fatty cheese, meat and other milk-based product to create sauces, along with oil-griddles meats and seafood. For instance, an extra helping of parmesan cheese in which a table spoon contains a gram of saturated fat can easily be avoided. Stay away from cannelloni, lasagna, ravioli and tortellini. These dishes are usually filled with thick cheeses and fatty meat. Other dishes to avoid are antipasti, fritto misto (fried seafood and meat) and fried squid. Some other obvious exceptions are heavy sauces. Alfredo and carbonara sauces are incredibly rich in saturated fats. Avoid capicola (smoked pork), prosciutto, salami, pepperoni and sausage; these contain a lot of fat and sodium.

The most important foods to avoid to achieve the benefits of the Mediterranean diet are foods with added sugars, highly processed foods, and foods containing refined carbohydrates.

- Soft drinks, sweets, ice cream, and anything that contains sugar
- Refined grains, such as pasta and white bread
- Trans fats found in margarine and other processed foods
- Refined oils such as canola oil, soybean oil, and others
- Processed meat, such as sausage and hot dogs
- Highly processed foods, with labels such as "low fat" or "diet," or something that contains a long list of ingredients that sound like chemicals

A good rule of thumb is to stay away from foods that have been made in a factory. Eat natural, whole foods that look like food.

The Mediterranean Diet Pyramid

Many people are now curious about the food pyramid. Most people in the Mediterranean have long enjoyed better health because of the type of food they serve at their table. The people there do not see it as a diet, but as their way of living and eating.

Many people who try the Mediterranean diet have benefited from better health and better well-being, while consuming the types of foods recommended by the slimming pyramid. In other words, if you plan to follow this diet to lose weight or improve your health, you can expect that it will not be a major challenge. Indeed, most of the recipes you can follow on this type of diet are tasty. You will not only benefit from better health, but the recipes will also bring you the satisfaction you are looking for each time you sit down at your table.

The diet pyramid provides recommendations for the type of food you eat. It is said that the recommendations not only help you lose weight but can also promote the health of your heart, prevent cancer and enhance your youthful appearance.

Fruits and vegetables are at the bottom of the pyramid. This means that you have to consume this type of food more often (daily).

On the other hand, red meat is at the top of the pyramid. Consumption must be limited to 1-2 times per month.

The Mediterranean diet pyramid was developed based on the eating habits of long-living adults in the Mediterranean. It follows a general food pyramid guideline (not specific quantities) and encourages communal eating and an active lifestyle.

Base every meal around:
- Legumes/beans, whole grains, nuts (e.g., lentils, walnuts)

- Olive oil as the major source of fat (swap out margarine and butter!)
- Vegetables and fruits (the darker in color, the more antioxidants!)

Eat at least 2x/week:
- Fish, seafood

Eat moderate portions daily to weekly:
- Dairy, cheese, and eggs
- Poultry
- Red wine (typically with meals) Females: 1 glass/day Males: 2 glasses/day

Eat seldom:
- Sweets
- Saturated fat
- Red meat

Mediterranean Diet Tips

A Mediterranean diet can lead to a longer and healthier life. Switching to a Mediterranean diet is not difficult. **Here are some tips for adapting to this way of eating healthy and old:**

- Eat slowly and enjoy every bite. Fortunately, Mediterranean style dishes are generally rich in taste, so enjoying slowly is a pleasure.
- If you eat meat, focus on fish, chicken and poultry. Only eat red meat occasionally and in small portions.
- Eat vegetarian meals at least a few times a week.
- Add a generous salad of green leaves to each dinner.
- Do not avoid carbohydrates; eat whole-grain bread, pasta, rice and cereal.
- Eat legumes several times a week: beans and lentils in all their wonderful shapes.
- Eat fish (not fried) at least twice a week.
- Replace butter with olive oil.
- Avoid processed foods. Eat nuts, fruits, and seeds instead.
- Serve fruit instead of sweet desserts.
- Enjoy a glass of red wine daily.

The Mediterranean diet is a pleasant and healthy way to eat. Many individuals who opt for this way of eating say that they will never eat otherwise.

2-WEEK MEAL PLAN

DAY 1

Breakfast
- a fried egg
- whole-wheat bread
- grilled tomatoes

For more calories, add another egg or some toast with avocado.

Lunch
- 2 cups of mixed salad with cherry tomatoes and olives on the top and an olive oil and vinaigrette
- whole-wheat pita bread
- 2 ounces (oz) of hummus

Dinner
- Whole-grain pizza with grilled vegetables, tomato sauce, and low-fat cheese as toppings

For more calories, add grated chicken, ham, tuna or pine nuts.

DAY 2

Breakfast
- 1 cup Greek yogurt
- half cups of fruit, such as blueberries, raspberries or chopped nectarines

For extra calories, add 1 to 2 ounces of almonds or walnuts.

Lunch
- Whole-grain sandwich with grilled vegetables, such as zucchini, eggplant, peppers and onions

For more calorie content, spread hummus or avocado on bread before adding fodder.

Dinner
- a portion of baked cod or salmon fried with garlic and black pepper to add flavor
- roasted potato with olive oil and chives

DAY 3

Breakfast
- 1 cup oatmeal with cinnamon, dates, and honey
- top with low sugar fruits such as raspberries
- 1 oz grated almonds (optional)

Lunch
- white beans cooked with spices such as laurel, garlic, and cumin
- 1 cup arugula with olive oil vinaigrette and tomato, cucumber and feta garnish

Dinner
- half cups of whole-wheat pasta with tomato sauce, olive oil, and grilled vegetables
- 1 tablespoon of parmesan cheese

DAY 4

Breakfast
- two scrambled eggs with peppers, onions, and tomatoes
- top with 1-ounce fresh cheese or one-quarter of an avocado

Lunch
- roasted anchovies in olive oil on whole-wheat bread with a pinch of lemon juice
- a boiled salad with 2 cups of steamed kale and tomatoes

Dinner
- 2 cups of steamed spinach with a pinch of lemon juice and herbs
- an artichoke cooked in olive oil, garlic powder, and salt

Add another artichoke for a hearty and filling meal.

DAY 5

Breakfast
- 1 cup of Greek yogurt with honey on top and cinnamon
- stir in a chopped apple and grated almonds

Lunch
- 1 cup of quinoa with peppers, sun-dried tomatoes, and olives
- roasted chickpeas with oregano and thyme
- garnish with feta cheese or avocado bread crumbs (optional)

Dinner

- 2 cups steamed cabbage with tomato, cucumber, olives, lemon juice, and parmesan
- a portion of roasted sardines with a slice of lemon

DAY 6

Breakfast

- two slices of whole-wheat toast with soft cheese such as ricotta cheese, fresh cheese or goat cheese
- add cranberries or chopped figs for more sweetness

Lunch

- 2 cups of vegetables mixed with cucumber and tomato
- a small portion of grilled chicken with a pinch of olive oil and lemon juice

Dinner

- Fried vegetables **such as:**
  - ✔ artichoke
  - ✔ carrot
  - ✔ zucchini
  - ✔ eggplant
  - ✔ sweet potato
  - ✔ tomato
- add olive oil and herbs for frying
- 1 cup of whole-grain couscous

DAY 7

Breakfast

- oatmeal with cinnamon, dates and maple syrup
- top with low sugar fruits such as raspberries or blackberries

Lunch

- Stewed zucchini, yellow squash, onions, and potatoes with tomato and herbs

Dinner

- 2 cups of vegetables, such as arugula or spinach, with tomatoes, olives, and olive oil.
- a small portion of white fish
- leftover vegetable stew from lunch

DAY 8

Breakfast

- Coffee or tea and two eggs with fried vegetables (spinach or kale), plus an orange
- **Snack:** Grilled chickpeas

Lunch

- Leftover lamb stew from dinner of day 6
- **Snack:** nuts mixed with a piece of dark chocolate

Dinner

- Fried white fish, roasted potatoes and zucchini

DAY 9

Breakfast

- Smoothie consisting of frozen cherries and banana pieces, cocoa powder and a choice of your preferred milk source.
- **Snack:** Mini peppers stuffed with hummus

Lunch

- Tuna salad with olive oil, dried herbs, olives, and sun-dried tomatoes served on a bed of spinach with a mixture of vegetables and whole-grain crackers
- **Snack:** A piece of cheese with a fruit

Dinner

- Tuscan white bean soup with whole-grain bread

DAY 10

Breakfast

- A bowl of oatmeal sprinkled with raisins and crushed nuts served with tea or coffee
- **Snack:** Greek yogurt and fruit

Lunch

- Leftover white bean Tuscan soup with from yesterday's dinner
- **Snack:** Hummus with sliced raw vegetables such as red pepper, celery, and cucumber

Dinner

- Lemon and garlic chicken legs with asparagus and Israeli couscous

DAY 11

Breakfast
- Coffee or tea and a slice of the vegetarian frittata with avocado
- **Snack:** Apple with walnut butter

Lunch
- Prepared dolmas (look for these stuffed grape leaves in the prepared foods section of some supermarkets) with hummus and pita
- **Snack:** Greek yogurt sauce with sliced vegetables

Dinner
- Seafood stew (white fish made from shrimps and tomatoes)

DAY 12

Breakfast
- Coffee or tea and a small bowl of ricotta covered with fruit (fresh berries, peaches, or apricots) and a pinch of honey.
- **Snack:** Handful of lightly salted nuts (pistachios, hazelnuts, almonds or a mixture)

Lunch
- Greek pasta salad (whole wheat pasta with red onions, tomatoes, Kalamata olives, and feta cheese) served on a bed of romaine lettuce
- **Snack:** Fruit salad

Dinner
- Leftover seafood stew from yesterday's dinner

DAY 13

Breakfast
- Coffee or tea and oatmeal with walnuts and blueberry butter
- **Snack:** 1 cup of Greek yogurt with fruit

Lunch
- Salmon salad with a cup of bean soup
- **Snack:** crushed avocado in biscuits

Dinner
- Shakshuka (eggs cooked in tomato sauce) topped with feta cheese and served on polenta

DAY 14

Breakfast
- Coffee or tea and whole wheat bread covered with ricotta and sliced fruit
- **Snack:** Dried cranberries and mixed nuts

Lunch
- Bowl of quinoa with roasted sweet potatoes, goat cheese, and walnuts
- **Snack:** Olives and some chopped fries in hummus

Dinner
- Cannellini artichoke and bean paste with bread crumbs and Parmesan cheese

CHAPTER 1: SMOOTHIES & BREAKFAST RECIPES

Preparing your favorite smoothie is a great way to start the day. It is recommended to eat five servings of fruits and vegetables a day. Preparing smoothies can be a quick and easy way to do this. Smoothies are rich in nutrients; they will provide your body with the minerals and vitamins it needs. Smoothies can be used as detox drinks; a smoothie diet can help you lose weight or help your body to function in the best possible way with a delicious fresh smoothie every day.

Smoothies are easy to make; you do not need more than 10 minutes to make a delicious and nutritious smoothie. Smoothies can be prepared with different kinds of fresh fruits and vegetables to which you can add herbs, nuts, and seeds, honey, different types of milk, or tea. There are countless smoothie recipes that you can find and try, but you can experiment and make your perfect smoothie.

5-ingredient Breakfast Smoothies

01. Mango Smoothie

Prep time: 3 minutes

Servings: 2

Ingredients

- 2 cups of fresh or frozen mangoes
- 1 un/frozen banana
- 1/2 cup milk
- 1/2 cup yogurt
- ⅛ cup unsweetened coconut

Instructions
1. Add all the ingredients in a powerful blender and blend until smooth.

Macros

Calories:329.6kcal, **Carbohydrates:**64.5g, **Protein:**6.3g, **Fat:**8.6g, **Saturated Fat:** 1.5g, **Sodium:** 27.7mg, **Fiber:** 7.2g, **Sugar:** 53.1g

02. Beetroot Smoothie

Prep time: 4 minutes

Servings: 1

Ingredients

- ½ apple (e.g., Golden Delicious)
- 1 small beetroot, pre-cooked
- ½ lime (juiced)
- 1 tsp maple syrup
- 10 mint, fresh, and 1¼ cups water

Instructions
1. Put everything into the blender. Enjoy!

Macros

Calories: 95,**Fat:** 1g,**Cholesterol:** 2mg, **Carbohydrates:** 19g, **Fiber:** 4g,**Sugar:** 13g,

Protein: 4g

03. Avocado Smoothie

Prep time: 5 minutes

Servings: 2

Ingredients

- ½ avocado
- 3 celery stalks
- 1 lime
- Fresh mint leaves
- 1 tsp linseeds

Instructions
1. Add all ingredients to a blender and blend until smooth.
2. Better when it's cool, you can keep the smoothie in the refrigerator for 1 to 2 days in an airtight container.

Macros

Calories: 178, **Sugar:** 8g, **Sodium:** 105mg, **Fat:** 11.6g, **Saturated fat:** 2.1g, **Carbohydrates:** 19.3g, **Fiber:** 5.7g, **Protein:** 2.5g

04. Red Smoothie

Prep time: 5 minutes

Servings: 1

Ingredients

- 2 cups mixed frozen red berries such as strawberries and raspberries
- 1 small red beet, peeled and thinly sliced
- 1 tablespoon fresh lemon juice
- 1 tablespoon honey
- 2 teaspoons unrefined extra-virgin coconut oil

Instructions

1. Put berries, 1/2 cup cold water, beets, lemon juice, honey, and coconut oil in a blender. Mix until smooth.
2. If necessary, add 1 to 2 more tablespoons of water to adjust the consistency.

Macros

Calories: 221, **Fat:** 1g, **Saturated Fat:** 0g, **Cholesterol:** 0mg, **Sodium:** 10mg, **Carbohydrates:** 56g, **Fiber:** 12g, **Sugar:** 33g, **Protein:** 3g

05. Green Smoothie

Prep time: 5 minutes

Servings: 2

Ingredients

- 1/2 cup yogurt, plain or Greek
- 2 cups kale, chopped
- 1 banana
- 1 cup pineapple, chopped
- 1 tablespoon flax seeds
- 1 cup milk
- honey to taste

Instructions

1. Add yogurt, kale, banana, pineapple, flaxseed, and milk in a blender.
2. Blend until smooth.
3. Add honey to taste. Serve immediately.

Macros

Calories: 240, **Fat:** 6g, **Saturated Fat:** 2g, **Cholesterol:** 13mg, **Sodium:** 108mg, **Potassium:** 942mg, **Carbohydrates:** 40g, **Fiber:** 4g, **Sugar:** 24g, **Protein:** 10g, **Vitamin A:** 7070%, **Vitamin C:** 125%, **Calcium:** 346%, **Iron:** 1.7%

06. Kale Smoothie

Prep time: 3 minutes

Servings: 1

Ingredients

- 2 cups of kale leaves
- 1 cup of almond milk
- 1 banana
- 1 apple
- cinnamon

Instructions

1. Blend all ingredients in a high-speed blender and blend until smooth. You may need a lid

and scrape the blender walls to blend everything together. Pour into a glass and serve immediately!

Macros

Total Calories: 187

Fat: 9g, of which **Saturated Fat:** 1g, **Cholesterol:** 3mg

Sodium: 149mg

Carbohydrates: 27g, of which **Sugar:** 13g, **Fiber:** 4g

Protein: 8g

07. Melon Smoothie

Prep time: 5 minutes

Servings: 2

Ingredients

- 1/4 cantaloupe - peeled, seeded and cubed
- 1/4 honeydew melon - peeled, seeded and cubed
- 1 lime, juiced
- 3 fresh mint leaves
- 2 tablespoons sugar

Instructions

1. Combine cantaloupe, honeydew, lime juice, and sugar in a blender. Blend until smooth. Pour into glasses and serve.

Macros

Calories: 70, **Fat:** 0.2g, **Carbohydrates:** 18.1g, **Protein:** 0.8g, **Cholesterol:** 0mg, **Sodium:** 20mg.

08. Pineapple Smoothie

Prep time: 5 minutes

Servings: 2

Ingredients

- ½ cup of fresh pineapple
- ½ cup of strawberry
- 1 banana
- ¼ cup of orange juice
- mint ice cubes

Instructions

1. Place the pineapple juice, banana, frozen pineapple, and vanilla Greek yogurt in a blender.
2. Blend until smooth.
3. Pour into 2 glasses. Garnish with pineapple wedges and mint sprigs if desired.

Macros

Calories: 169kcal, **Carbohydrates:** 33g, **Protein:** 6g, **Cholesterol:** 2mg, **Sodium:** 33mg, **Potassium:** 744mg, **Fiber:** 7g, **Sugar:** 35g, **Vitamin A:** 250IU, **Vitamin C:** 62.7mg, Calcium: 91mg, **Iron:** 1.9mg.

09. Kiwi Smoothie

Prep time: 5 minutes

Servings: 2-3

Ingredients

- 5 kiwi, peeled and cut into chunks
- ½ cup of fresh pineapple
- 1 banana, cut into 4 pieces and frozen
- basil leaves
- 1 cup frozen blueberries
- 1 cup fat-free plain yogurt
- 3 tablespoons honey
- 1/4 teaspoon almond extract
- 1-1/2 cups crushed ice

Instructions

1. Combine the kiwi, pineapple, banana, basil leaves, blueberries, yogurt, honey, and extract in a blender if desired; cover and process until combined.
2. Add ice; cover and process until blended. Stir if necessary. Pour into chilled glasses; serve immediately.

Macros

Calories: 196, **Fat:** 1g, Saturated fat: 0g, **Cholesterol:** 1mg, **Sodium:** 48mg, **Carbohydrate:** 46g, **Sugars:** 37g, **Fiber:** 5g, **Protein:** 5g.

10. Sweet Smoothie

Prep time: 5 minutes

Servings: 2

Ingredients

- 1 banana
- 1 sliced mango
- 1 cup fresh pineapple
- 1 tablespoon peanut butter, or more to taste
- ½ coconut water

Instructions

1. Process the banana, mango, pineapple, peanut butter, and coconut water in a blender until smooth and creamy.
2. Enjoy immediately or keep cool in the refrigerator.

Macros

Calories: 168; **Fat:** 0.7g; **Carbohydrates:** 42.3g; **Protein:** 1.5g; **Cholesterol:** 0mg; **Sodium:** 5mg.

11. Strawberry-Flax Smoothie

Prep time: 5 minutes

Servings: 1

Ingredients

- 1 cup of frozen strawberries
- ¾ cup plain low-fat yogurt
- ½ cup fresh orange juice
- 1 tablespoon honey
- 1 tablespoon flaxseed meal

Instructions

1. Combine the strawberries, yogurt, orange juice, honey, and flaxseed meal in a blender.
2. Blend until smooth.

Macros

Calories: 334, **Fat:** 7g, **Saturated fat:** 2g, **Cholesterol:** 11mg, **Sodium:** 134mg, **Protein:** 14g, **Carbohydrate:** 58g, **Sugar:** 49g, **Fiber:** 6g, **Iron:** 2mg, **Calcium:** 391mg

12. Coconut Milk Smoothie

Prep time: 5 minutes

Servings: 4

Ingredients

- 1 10-ounce bag frozen blueberries or other fruit
- 1 cup plain yogurt
- 3 ripe bananas
- 1 cup unsweetened coconut milk
- 2 tablespoons honey

Instructions

1. Combine the blueberries, bananas, yogurt, coconut milk, and honey in a blender and serve.

Macros

Calories: 300, **Calories from fat:** 41%, **Fat:** 15g, **Saturated fat:** 12g, **Cholesterol:** 10mg, **Sodium:** 40mg, **Carbohydrate:** 43g, **Fiber:** 3g, **Sugar:** 28g, **Protein:** 5g

13. Raspberry Chia Smoothie

Prep time: 5 minutes
Servings: 1
Ingredients

- 1 cup frozen raspberries
- ¾ cup apple juice
- ½ cup plain yogurt
- 1 banana
- 1 tablespoon chia seeds
- ½ teaspoon pure vanilla extract (optional)

Instructions

1. Place the raspberries, apple juice, yogurt, banana, chia seeds, and vanilla, if desired, in a blender.
2. Blend until smooth.

Macros

Calories: 413, **Fat:** 10g, **Saturated fat:** 3g, **Cholesterol:** 16mg, **Sodium:** 79mg, **Protein:** 10g, **Carbohydrate:** 77g, **Sugar:** 49g, **Fiber:** 15g, **Iron:** 3mg, **Calcium:** 284mg

14. Spiced Pumpkin Smoothie

Prep time: 5 minutes
Servings: 1
Ingredients

- 1 cup ice
- ½ cup whole milk
- ⅓ cup pure pumpkin puree
- 1 tablespoon honey
- Pinch of ground nutmeg

Instructions

1. Place the ice, milk, pumpkin puree, honey, and nutmeg in a blender.
2. Blend until smooth.

Macros

Calories: 165, **Fat:** 4g, **Saturated fat:** 2g, **Cholesterol:** 12mg, **Sodium:** 53mg, **Protein:** 5g, **Carbohydrate:** 29g, **Sugar:** 26g, **Fiber:** 3g, **Iron:** 1mg, **Calcium:** 153mg

05. Carrot-Pineapple Smoothie

Prep time: 5 minutes
Servings: 2
Ingredients

- ¾ cup chopped fresh pineapple
- ½ cup ice

- ⅓ cup fresh orange juice
- ¼ cup chopped carrot
- ½ banana

Instructions

1. Place the pineapple, ice, orange juice, carrot, and banana in a blender.
2. Blend until smooth.

Macros

Calories: 159, **Fat:** 1g, **Saturated fat:** 0g, **Cholesterol:** 0mg, **Sodium:** 25mg, **Protein:** 2g, **Carbohydrate:** 40g, **Sugar:** 26g, **Fiber:** 4g, **Iron:** 1mg, **Calcium:** 38mg

16. Tropical Green Chia Seed Smoothie

Prep time: 5 minutes
Servings: 1
Ingredients

- 1 cup loosely packed chopped kale
- 3/4 cup frozen pineapple chunks
- 1/2 cup frozen mango
- 1/3 small banana frozen
- 1/3 cup silk unsweetened almond milk
- 1 small orange peeled
- 2 teaspoons chia seeds

Instructions

1. Add ingredients into a food processor until blended.
2. Serve immediately.

Macros

Calories: 291kcal, **Carbohydrates:** 62g, **Protein:** 7g, **Fat:** 4g, **Sodium:** 137mg, **Potassium:** 980mg, **Fiber:** 9g, **Sugar:** 40g, **Vitamin A:** 7955IU, **Vitamin C:** 242.7mg, **Calcium:** 319mg, **Iron:** 2mg

17. Blueberry Spinach Breakfast Smoothie

Prep time: 5 minutes
Servings: 2
Ingredients

- 3 tablespoons old-fashioned oats
- 1 cup fresh spinach
- 1 cup frozen blueberries
- 1/3 cup plain Greek yogurt
- ¾ cup milk
- 1/8 teaspoon cinnamon

Instructions

1. Place all the ingredients in a blender and blend until smooth. Serve immediately.

Macros

Calories: 168kcal, **Carbohydrates:** 26g, **Protein:** 9g, **Fat:** 4g, **Saturated Fat:** 2g, **Cholesterol:** 10mg, **Sodium:** 73mg, **Fiber:** 4g, **Sugar:** 16g

18. Peanut Butter Banana Smoothie

Prep time: 5 minutes
Servings: 2
Ingredients

- ¾ cup of ice cubes
- 1 medium banana peeled, cut into chunks and frozen
- ¾ cup Greek yogurt
- ½ cup milk
- 2 tablespoons peanut butter

Instructions

1. Add ingredients into a food processor until blended.
2. Enjoy immediately.

Macros

Calories: 456kcal, **Carbohydrates**: 44g, **Protein**: 28g, **Fat:** 21g, **Saturated Fat:** 5g, **Cholesterol:** 19mg, **Sodium**: 255mg, **Potassium:** 1002mg, **Fiber:** 4g, **Sugar:** 28g, **Vitamin A:** 275IU, **Vitamin C:** 10.2mg, **Calcium:** 317mg, **Iron:** 0.9mg

19. Cocoa Almond Protein Smoothie

Prep time: 5 minutes
Servings: 2
Ingredients

- 1/2 cup plus 2 tbsp. milk almond, dairy, etc.
- 4 tablespoons almond butter
- 1 tablespoon unsweetened cocoa powder
- 1.5 cup Greek yogurt
- 2 medium banana sliced and frozen
- 1.5 cup ice cubes
- 4 teaspoons ground flaxseed

Instructions

1. Place all the ingredients in a blender and blend until smooth. Enjoy!

Macros

Calories: 471kcal, **Carbohydrates:** 45g, **Protein:** 27g, **Fat:** 23g, **Saturated Fat:** 3g, **Cholesterol:** 16mg, **Sodium:** 98mg, **Potassium:** 1030mg, **Fiber:** 8g, **Sugar:** 25g, **Vitamin A:** 220IU, **Vitamin C:** 10.2mg, **Calcium:** 388mg, **Iron:** 2mg

20. Pumpkin Smoothie

Prep time: 5 minutes
Servings: 2
Ingredients

- ¼ cup plus 2 tablespoons old-fashioned oats
- ¼ cup canned pumpkin puree
- ¾ cup plain Greek yogurt
- 1 medium apple cut into pieces
- ½ small banana sliced and frozen
- ½ cup ice cubes
- 1/8 teaspoon pumpkin pie spice
- ½ cup milk

Instructions

1. Put the oatmeal in a blender and blend for about 30 seconds until it is finely chopped.
2. Add remaining ingredients and blend until smooth. Serve immediately.

Macros

Calories: 187kcal,
Carbohydrates: 32g, of which **Sugar:** 15g
Protein: 11g, **Fat:** 2g, **Cholesterol:** 6mg,
Sodium: 58mg, **Fiber:** 6g,

21. Peanut Butter Banana Smoothie

Prep time: 5 minutes
Servings: 4
Ingredients

- 2 bananas, broken into chunks
- 2 cups of milk
- 1/2 cup peanut butter
- 2 tablespoons honey
- 2 cups of ice cubes

Instruction

1. Put bananas, milk, peanut butter, honey, and ice cubes in a blender; mix until smooth, about 30 seconds.

Macros

Per serving: 335 calories; 18.8 g of fat; 34.1 g carbohydrates; 12.8 g of protein; 10 mg cholesterol; 203 mg of sodium.

22. Groovy Green Smoothie

Prep time: 10 minutes
Servings: 2
Ingredients

- 1 banana, cut in chunks
- 1 cup grapes
- 1 (6 ounces) tub vanilla yogurt
- 1/2 apple, cored and chopped
- 1 1/2 cups fresh spinach leaves

Instructions

1. Put the banana, grapes, yogurt, apple, and spinach in a blender. Cover and mix until smooth.
2. Pour into glasses and serve.

Macros

Per serving: 205 calories; 1.9 g fat; 45 g carbohydrates; 6.1 g of protein; 4 mg cholesterol; 76 mg of sodium.

23. Pineapple and Banana Smoothie

Prep time: 5 minutes
Servings: 1
Ingredients

- 4 ice cubes
- 1/4 fresh pineapple - cored, peeled, and cubed
- 1 large banana, cut into chunks
- 1 cup pineapple or apple juice

Instructions

1. Place the ice cubes, pineapple, bananas, and pineapple juice in the bowl of a blender. Puree smooth.

Macros

Per serving: 0.9 g fat; 313 calories; 78.7 g of carbohydrates; 3 g of protein; 0 mg of cholesterol; 10 mg of sodium.

24. Oatmeal and Strawberry Breakfast Smoothie

Prep time: 5 minutes
Servings: 2
Ingredients

- 1 cup of soy milk
- 1/2 cup oatmeal
- 1 banana cut into pieces
- 14 frozen strawberries
- 1/2 teaspoon vanilla extract
- 1 1/2 teaspoon of white sugar

Instructions

1. Combine soy milk, oats, banana, and strawberries in a blender.
2. Add vanilla and sugar if you want. Mix until smooth. Pour into glasses and serve.

Macros

Per serving: 236 calories; 3.7 g of fat; 44.9 g carbohydrates; 7.6 g of protein; 0 mg of cholesterol; 65 mg of sodium.

25. Sun Juice

Prep time: 10 minutes
Servings: 1
Ingredients

- 2 oranges, peeled and sliced
- 1/2 cup fresh raspberries
- 1 medium-sized banana, peeled
- 3 fresh mint leaves

Instructions

1. Juice everything in the juice machine. Pour on the ice to serve.

Macros

Per serving: 293 calories; 1.1 g of fat; 73.6 g carbohydrates; 5 g of protein; 0 mg of cholesterol; 1 mg of sodium

26. Creamy Banana Strawberry Split Smoothie

Prep time: 10 minutes
Servings: 4
Ingredients

- 1 cup almond milk
- 1 chopped banana
- 3/4 cup strawberries
- 3 ice cubes
- 1 tablespoon vanilla protein powder 1, 1 teaspoon vanilla extract, 1 teaspoon honey
- 1 teaspoon ground flaxseed, 1 teaspoon ground chia seed,
- 1/2 teaspoon of ground cinnamon

Instructions

1. Mix almond milk, bananas, strawberries, ice cubes, protein powder, vanilla extract, honey, ground linseed, ground chia seeds, and cinnamon to a smooth mass.

Macros

Per serving: 111 calories; 1.6 g of fat; 14.4 g carbohydrates; 10.4 g of protein; 3 mg cholesterol; 95 mg of sodium.

27. Peach Juice with Mint

Prep time: 5 minutes
Servings: 1
Ingredients
2. 3 large peaches or nectarines, diced
3. 1 large apple, in quarters
4. 1 lime
5. 2 sprigs of fresh mint

Instructions
1. Squeeze the peaches, apples, and lime into a juice. Pour the juice into a blender with the mint leaves. Mix.

Macros
Per serving: 0.5 g fat; 60.8 g carbohydrates; 232 calories; 1.3 g of protein; 0 mg cholesterol; 19 mg of sodium.

28. Matcha Coconut Smoothie

Prep time: 10 minutes
Servings: 1
Ingredients
2. 1 banana, 1 cup frozen mango chunks
3. 2 leaves kale, torn into several pieces
4. 3 tablespoons white beans, drained
5. 2 tablespoons unsweetened shredded coconut
6. 1 cup water, 1/2 teaspoon matcha green tea powder

Instructions
1. Place the ingredients in the blender, add water and blend until smooth.

Macros
Per serving: 367 calories; 8.8 g fat; 72.4 g carbohydrates; 8 g protein; 0 mg cholesterol; 36 mg sodium.

29. Gloomy Day Smoothie

Prep time: 10 minutes
Servings: 4
Ingredients
2. 1 mango - seeded, peeled, and cut into pieces
3. 1 banana, peeled and chopped
4. 1 cup of orange juice
5. 1 cup vanilla yogurt

Instructions
1. Put the mango, banana, orange juice, and yogurt in a blender. Mix until smooth. Serve in clear glasses and drink with a soft straw!

Macros
Per serving: 0.5 g fat;151 calories; 34.6 g carbohydrates; 4.2 g of protein; <1 mg cholesterol; 44 mg of sodium.

30. Orange Chocolate Breakfast Drink

Prep time: 10 minutes
Servings: 1
Ingredients
- 1 orange - peeled, quartered and cut into pieces
- 1/2 inch slices
- 2 tablespoons chocolate syrup
- 1 cup of cold milk
- 1 cup crushed ice

Instructions
1. Mix the orange slices, chocolate syrup, milk, and ice in a blender. Mix until smooth. Transfer into a large glass and enjoy it.

Macros
Per serving: 306 calories; 5.4 g of fat; 55.6 g carbohydrates; 10.4 g of protein; 20 mg of cholesterol; 135 mg of sodium.

31. Supercharged Smoothie

Prep time: 10 minutes
Servings: 1
Ingredients
- 1/2 cup fresh papaya, 1 cup almond milk
- 1 tablespoon protein powder
- 1 piece of chopped and fresh turmeric root peeled
- 1 piece of fresh ginger root, peeled
- 3 ice cubes or as desired

Instructions
1. In a blender, mix almond milk, papaya, protein powder, turmeric, and ginger root. Add the ice and mix until smooth.

Macros
Per serving: 207 calories; 3.8 grams of fat; 24.8 g carbohydrates; 17.4 g of protein; 0 mg of cholesterol; 348 mg of sodium.

32. BFF Smoothie

Prep time: 10 minutes
Servings: 2

Ingredients

- 1 cup frozen mango chunks
- 1/2 cup of milk
- 1 cup plain Greek yogurt
- 1 cup of frozen strawberries
- 5 fresh mint leaves
- 1 tablespoon vanilla-whey protein powder

Instructions

1. Mix the strawberries, Greek yogurt, mango, milk, and protein powder to obtain a smooth consistency.
2. Add the mint leaves and beat until the leaves are chopped, 4 to 5 pulses.

Macros

Per serving: 335 calories; 11.6 g of fat; 33 grams of carbohydrates 27.7 g of protein; 32 mg of cholesterol; 202 mg of sodium.

33. Yam Smoothie

Prep time: 5 minutes
Servings: 8

Ingredients

- 2 medium-sized yams
- 3 cups vanilla yogurt
- 1 cup of milk
- 2 cups of ice cubes
- 1 teaspoon of white sugar
- 1 ripe banana, sliced

Instructions

1. Prick the sweet potatoes with a fork and place them on a plate. Microwave for 8 to 10 minutes, turning once, until soft. Cool, peel, and cut into cubes.
2. Combine yams, yogurt, milk, ice cubes, sugar, and banana in a blender jar. Mix until smooth.

Macros

Per serving: 226 calories; 2 grams of fat; 45.9 g carbohydrates; 7.2 g of protein; 7 mg of cholesterol;

84 mg of sodium.

34. Gordon's Berry Breakfast Drink

Prep time: 5 minutes
Servings: 6

Ingredients

- 3/4 cup chilled orange juice
- 1/3 cup chilled pineapple juice
- 2 cups vanilla yogurt
- 1 cup of frozen blueberries
- 1/2 cup of frozen strawberries
- 1/2 banana, sliced

Instructions

1. Put the orange juice, pineapple juice, yogurt, blueberries, strawberries, and bananas in a blender.
2. Cover and mix until smooth. The berry drink will be very thick. Serve immediately.

Macros

Per serving: 1.2 g fat; 120 calories; 23.7 g of carbohydrates; 4.7 g of protein; 4 mg cholesterol; 55 mg of sodium

35. Tofu berry Smoothie

Prep time: 7 minutes
Servings: 3

Ingredients

- ¼ cup diced silken tofu
- 2 tablespoons soy milk
- ¼ cup fruit yogurt
- ½ cup raspberries
- ¼ banana, 2 cups orange juice

Instructions

1. Place tofu, soy milk, yogurt, raspberries, banana, and orange juice in a blender. Blend until smooth. Pour in glasses over ice or vanilla ice cream.

Macros

Per serving: 132 calories; 1.4 g total fat; 1 mg cholesterol; 26 mg sodium. 26.8 g carbohydrates; 4.1 g protein;

CHAPTER 2: ANTIPASTI & SMALL PLATES

Antipasti, the food offered before the start of the meal, is a colorful and delicious way to prepare the scene for the next party and invite your friends and family to the table. In the Italian tradition, antipasti are selected for their color, taste, texture, and complementarity with the food to come. Antipasti have become a social event in their own right, with an entertaining role in the gastronomic scene.

Here are some antipasti and small plates recipes that are easy to prepare:

36. Calamari Fritti

Prep time: 20 minutes

Servings: 4

Ingredients

- 1 lb. squid rings (about 450 grams) (cut the squid into rings)
- A neutral-flavored oil with a high smoke point for frying (such as peanut oil or refined coconut oil)
- 4 medium eggs
- 2/3 cup unbleached flour for all purposes
- 4 tablespoons semolina
- 1 lemon (cut into pieces)
- fine salt

Instructions

1. Rinse the squid pieces under running water and dry thoroughly with paper towels.
2. Heat a few inches of the oil in a large, high-walled pan with a thick bottom over medium heat or 350°F.
3. Place the flour in a shallow bowl. Beat the eggs lightly in a large bowl.
4. Place the semolina in a small bowl. Dip the squid rings in the flour and shake them to remove the excess. Dip in the egg and then in the semolina before frying them in the hot oil.
5. Bake in different batches to avoid overcrowding until you get a crisp, light brown texture, about one or two minutes.
6. Transfer the fried squid to a dish with absorbent paper to drain. Season with salt and serve with lemon slices. Enjoy!

Macros

Calories: 333, **Fat:** 11g, **Carbohydrates:** 29g, **Protein:** 29g

37. Arancini

Prep time: 1 hour and 50 minutes

Servings: 16

Ingredients

- 3 cups low sodium chicken broth
- kosher salt
- 1 cup arborio rice
- 2 tablespoons grilled pine nuts
- 1/2 cup grated mozzarella cheese (2 ounces)
- 1/2 cup grated Fontina cheese (2 ounces)
- 2 tablespoons chopped fresh parsley
- 2 large eggs
- 1/2 cup grated parmesan
- 1 1/2 cups bread crumbs
- vegetable oil for frying

Instructions

1. Add ¼ teaspoon of salt to the chicken broth in a medium-sized saucepan over medium heat. When broth starts to boil, add the rice and immediately reduce the heat to allow it to simmer for about 20 minutes. Spread on a baking sheet lined with parchment paper and allow to cool completely.
2. Mix the pine nuts, mozzarella, fontina and parsley in a bowl; set aside.
3. Beat the eggs in a large bowl, then add the cold rice, parmesan, and 2/3 cup of breadcrumbs. Form the mixture into sixteen 1 1/2-inch balls.
4. Place the rest of the breadcrumbs in a shallow bowl. Press your finger in the center of each rice ball, add 2 teaspoons of the mozzarella lamb mixture and squeeze the rice around the filling to wrap it. Roll the meatballs into the bread crumbs and place them on a baking sheet lined with parchment paper. Cover and refrigerate without pinching for at least 1 hour or overnight. (If you cool at night, roll more bread crumbs before frying).
5. Heat 1/2-inch vegetable oil in a big saucepan over medium heat until a frying thermometer detects 350°F. Work in portions, fry the rice balls, and flip them on all sides until they are golden for about 4 minutes. Remove with a spoon with a slit and drain on paper towels; season with salt.

Macros

Calories: 252; **Fat:** 16.4g; **Carbohydrates:** 18.8g;

Protein: 6.3g; **Cholesterol:** 29mg; **Sodium:** 274mg

38. "Al Taglio" Roman Style Street Pizza

Prep time: 15 minutes

Servings: 8

Ingredients

- 4 medium-sized heritage tomatoes
- 1 jar of marinated artichoke hearts
- 8 oz Fontina, sliced
- 8 oz ham, sliced
- 1/2 packet of arugula
- 1 fresh mozzarella
- pinch of salt
- pinch of pepper
- extra virgin olive oil

For the Pizza Dough

- 4 cups of all-purpose flour and more to roll
- 1/4 teaspoon of instant dry yeast
- 2 teaspoons of kosher salt or 1 teaspoon of sea salt
- 1 1/2 cups water 110 degrees F

Instructions

For the Pizza Dough

1. Combine salt and 1/4 cup of water in a large bowl.
2. Combine the yeast in a small bowl with 1/4 cup more water. Mix to dissolve the yeast and set aside completely.
3. Add 1/2 cup of flour with saltwater and stir to incorporate.
4. Add the rest of the flour, stir and add the yeast mixture.
5. Stir the rest of the water until the dough forms a ball. If the dough is sticky, add an extra quantity of flour, 1 tablespoon at a time, until the dough is combined into a firm ball. If the dough is too dry, add a little more water, 1 tablespoon at a time.
6. Knead in a softball and firm, cover with plastic wrap and let rise for 24 hours.
7. Preheat the oven to 350°F.
8. Place a cooling rack on a large baking sheet and brush with olive oil.
9. Place the tomato slices ontop and season with salt, pepper and drizzle a generous amount of olive oil.

10. Bake until tomatoes are tender, about 15 minutes.
11. Cover a 22 x 16-inch baking sheet with 1 tablespoon of olive oil. Transfer the dough to the sheet. Press the dough with your fingertips to hold on the baking sheet. Let the dough rest for 10 minutes. Sprinkle with 2 tablespoons of olive oil.

Baking

1. Preheat the oven to 450°F.
2. Cover the left side of the dough with cooled roasted tomatoes, the center part with the artichokes, and the right side with the fontina and ham. Bake pizza for 15 minutes or until the crust is golden, and ingredients are bubbling and melting.
3. Spread the arugula and pieces of fresh mozzarella on the center part. Cut into rectangular pieces and serve hot.

Macros

Calories: 441kcal, **Carbohydrates:** 51g, **Protein:** 20 g, **Fat:** 16g, of which **Saturated fat:** 7g, **Cholesterol:** 50mg,

Sodium: 1232mg, **Potassium:** 311mg, **Fiber:** 2g, **Sugar:** 2g, **Vitamin A:** 985 IU, **Vitamin C:** 12.9mg, **Calcium:** 179mg, **Iron:** 3.5mg

39. Parmesan Sandwiches

Prep time: 25 minutes

Servings: 2

Ingredients

- 1/2 cup all-purpose flour
- 1 large egg lightly beaten
- 3/4 cup of breadcrumbs
- 3 tablespoons grated parmesan cheese
- 2 boneless and skinless chicken breast halves (5 ounces each)
- 1/8 teaspoon salt
- 1/8 teaspoon pepper
- 2 tablespoons of olive oil
- 2 Italian bread rolls, divided
- 2 slices of provolone cheese
- 1/3 cup of marinara sauce or other meatless pasta sauce, heated

Instructions

1. Place the flour and egg in separate, shallow containers. Mix the breadcrumbs in another bowl with parmesan cheese.

2. Pound the chicken with ½-in. wooden hammer. Thickness Sprinkle with salt and pepper. Dip the chicken in the flour to cover both sides; shake off the excess. Dip the egg into the crumb mixture.

3. Heat the oil in a large frying pan over medium heat. Add the chicken; Bake until chicken is golden and chicken is no longer pink, 4 to 5 minutes per side. Serve in sandwiches with provolone cheese and sauce.

Macros

Calories: 669, **Fat:** 32g, **Saturated fat:** 10g, **Cholesterol:** 198mg, **Sodium:** 1124mg, **Carbohydrates:** 45g, **Sugars:** 3g, **Fiber:** 3g, **Protein:** 48g.

40. Roasted Red Pepper and Fresh Mozzarella

Prep time: 20 minutes

Servings: 4

Ingredients

- 1 bowl of fresh mozzarella
- 1/4 cup of quality olive oil
- 1/4 cup basil leaves, julienned
- 1 large red pepper
- Salt and pepper to taste

Instructions

1. Mix ingredients and enjoy!

Macros

Calories: 166; **Fat:** 13g; **Saturated fat:** 5g; **Fiber:** 1g; **Carbohydrates:** 9g; **Protein:** 6g; **Cholesterol:** 7mg; **Sugars:** 5g; **Vitamin A:** 543 IU; **Vitamin C:** 219mg; **Calcium:** 117mg; **Iron:** 1mg; **Sodium:** 307mg; **Potassium:** 259mg

41. Antipasto Platter

Prep time: 10 minutes

Servings: 8

Ingredients

- 1 jar (24 grams) of pepperoncini, drained
- 1 can (15 grams) of chickpeas, rinsed and drained
- 2 cups fresh mushrooms, halved
- 2 cups of cherry tomatoes, halved
- 1/2 pound of provolone cheese, diced
- 1 can (6 grams) of drained ripe unripe olives

- 1 bottle (8 grams) of Italian vinaigrette
- Lettuce leaves

Instructions

1. Mix the pepperoncini, beans, mushrooms, tomatoes, cheese, and olives in a large bowl. Pour the vinaigrette on the mixture.

2. Cool for at least 30 minutes or overnight. Arrange in a bowl with lettuce. Serve with toothpicks.

Macros

Calories: 178, **Fat:** 13g, **Saturated fat:** 4g, **Cholesterol:** 15mg, **Sodium:** 852mg, **Carbohydrates:** 8g, **Sugars:** 2g, **Fiber:** 2g, **Protein:** 6g

42. Baked Polenta and Sausage

Prep time: 25 minutes

Servings: 4

Ingredients

- 5 1/2 tablespoons olive oil
- 1 can of crushed tomatoes
- 1 tbsp chopped fresh oregano
- 1 medium yellow onion, thinly sliced
- 1 medium-sized yellow, red or orange pepper, thinly sliced
- 2 garlic cloves, finely chopped
- 1/2 teaspoon salt
- freshly ground black pepper
- red pepper flakes
- 1-pound Italian sausage, sweet or spicy
- 2 tubes (16 ounces each) prepared polenta, sliced 1/2-inch-thick
- 8 oz fresh mozzarella, drained and sliced 1/4 inch

Instructions

1. Preheat the oven to 400° F. Heat the oil in a large frying pan over medium heat. Add the onion and fry for 5 minutes. Add the sausage and cook. Break the meat with a wooden spoon until golden brown, about 8 minutes. Add the garlic and cook until fragrant for 30 seconds. Remove the pan from the heat and add the artichokes. Season with salt and pepper.

2. Place the polenta layers and tablespoons of the sausage mixture in a two-quart gratin dish. Pour broth and cook until bubbling,

and polenta is golden 20 to 25 minutes. Sprinkle with parsley and serve.

Macros

Calories: 510, **Fat:** 30g, **Saturated fat:** 10g, **Cholesterol:** 82mg, **Sodium:** 1505mg, **Carbohydrates:** 33g, **Dietary fiber:** 4.8g, **Protein:** 23g

43. Baked Eggplant Rollatini

Prep time: 45 minutes

Servings: 5

Ingredients

- 2 medium-sized eggplants (about 1 pound each)
- 2 tablespoons canola oil
- 1 cup chopped yellow onion
- 1 1/2 cups low-sodium marinara sauce, divided
- 1 large egg
- 1 packet (15 oz). Frozen spinach, thawed and squeezed (about 1 1/4 cups)
- 1/2 cup of partially low-fat ricotta cheese
- 2 medium garlic cloves, finely chopped (2 teaspoons)
- ½ teaspoon of kosher salt
- 6 ounces of partially skimmed mozzarella cheese grated (about 1 1/2 cups), divided
- 2 tablespoons chopped fresh basil

Instructions

1. Sliced ends of the eggplant. Cut the eggplants lengthwise into 1/4-inch-thick slices, then discard the shell-covered ends. You should get about 16 slices in total. Place the slices on a rimmed baking sheet and sprinkle both sides with salt. Let stand 15 minutes, then rinse in cold water and dry the slices.

2. Preheat oven to 400° F. Brush the eggplant slices on both sides with olive oil and lay them in separate layers on 2 baking sheets. Roast for 15 minutes, until softened. Let the sheets cool on the rack until they are cold enough to handle.

3. Combine spinach, ricotta, garlic, eggs, 1/2 cup mozzarella, and 1/2 cup parmesan cheese in a large bowl. Season with 1 teaspoon salt and 1/2 teaspoon. pepper spray a 9 x 13-inch baking dish with an oil spray.

Spread 1/2 cup of sauce on the bottom of the plate. Divide the ricotta mixture over the eggplant slices, use about 1/3 cup for each, spread it in the middle. Roll the slices and place them with the seam in a baking dish. Cover with remaining sauce and sprinkle with remaining mozzarella and parmesan cheese.

4. Cover the baking dish with foil and bake for 30 minutes. Remove the foil and cook until golden and bubbly, about 15 minutes longer. Let cool 10 minutes before serving.

Macros

Calories: 316, **Fat:** 19g, **Saturated fat:** 6g, **Unsaturated fat:** 9g, **Protein:** 18g, **Carbohydrates:** 23g, **Fiber:** 8g, **Sugars:** 10g, **Sodium:** 697mg, **Calcium:** 45% DV, **Potassium:** 16% DV

44. Crispy Coconut Shrimp

Prep time: 25 minutes.

Servings: 8

Ingredients

- 3/4 cup all-purpose flour
- 3/4 cup corn flour
- 1 tablespoon baking powder
- 1/2 teaspoon of kosher salt
- 1/2 teaspoon of cayenne pepper
- 1 1/2 teaspoon of vegetable oil and more for frying
- 1 bag (7 oz) of sweet coconut flakes,
- 32 large shrimps (about 1 lb.), peeled to the tail
- 1 cup cocktail sauce

Instructions

1. Combine flour, cornflour, baking powder, salt, and pepper in a large bowl. Beat. Cool the water and oil until they are mixed, thick, and foamy. Set the dough aside.

2. Pour the oil about 1 1/2 inches deep into a large deep pan. Heat the oil to 375 ° F. Meanwhile, break the pieces of coconut and spread them on a baking sheet lined with waxed paper. Dry the shrimp with paper towels. Dip the shrimp in the dough one by one to cover them well; Shake off the excess and place it on the coconut. Roll each shrimp

in the coconut to cover; shake off the excess paper and transfer it to a rack.

3. Put the shrimp in hot oil, 6 to 8 at a time, and cook for about 1 minute or until golden and crisp; Adjust the heat to maintain the temperature at 375 ° F. Transfer shrimp with a wire mesh skimmer, drip spoon or tweezers to a baking sheet lined with paper towels to remove. Repeat this with the remaining shrimp and keep the oil as clean as possible by removing the waste with a skimmer or small sieve.

4. Place the shrimp in a bowl and serve hot with the cocktail sauce separately.

Macros

Calories: 317, **Fat:** 19.3g, **Carbohydrates:** 26.3g, **Protein:** 8.4g, **Cholesterol:** 67mg, **Sodium:** 241mg

45. Spiedini

Prep time: 55 minutes
Servings: 8

Ingredients

- 1 pound of finely sliced beef eye
- 1 cup crumbs
- 1 cup Roman pecorino
- 1/4 cup red berries
- 1/4 cup pine nuts
- 1/4 cup finely chopped fresh parsley
- bay leaves, dried or fresh
- salt and pepper
- 2 large onions
- extra virgin olive oil
- 1/4 cup cooked tomatoes

Instructions

1. Preheat the oven to 200° C. Heat 1/2 cup of olive oil and vegetable oil in a large frying pan (the oil should be 1 inch deep).

2. Place a piece of bread on the work surface. Cover with 2 slices of mozzarella. Cover with a second slice of bread. Repeat this with the rest of the bread and cheese to make a sandwich of several layers. Cut the sandwich into four equal parts and place a 10-inch skewer in the center of each. Carefully cut off the crusts and discard them.

3. Beat the eggs, milk, salt, and pepper and pour into a shallow baking dish. Coat the

rolls with flour and shake to remove the excess. Dip in the egg mixture. Place in hot oil. Bake, occasionally turning, until all sides are golden brown. Drain on a baking sheet lined with paper towels and put in the oven to keep warm.

4. Heat the remaining 2 teaspoons of olive oil in a medium frying pan over medium heat. Add garlic and fry until golden brown. Add the beef eye and cook stirring until they fall to pieces. Add white wine, lemon juice, and capers. Bring to boil vigorously and continue cooking until reduced by half.

5. Add the parsley to the reduced sauce. Remove the skewers from the rolls and serve them lightly with a sauce. Decorate with parsley sprigs.

Macros

Calories: 257, **Fat:** 17g, **Carbohydrates:** 23g, **Protein:** 9g, **Cholesterol:** 75mg, **Sodium:** 262mg

46. Curry Chicken Tikka Masala Sauce

Prep time: 15 minutes
Servings: 6

Ingredients

- 2 tablespoons ghee (clarified butter)
- 1 onion, finely chopped
- 4 cloves of garlic, minced
- 1 teaspoon ground ginger
- 1 tablespoon ground cumin
- 1 teaspoon cayenne pepper
- ½ teaspoon ground cinnamon
- ¼ teaspoon ground turmeric
- 1 can tomato sauce (14 oz)
- 1 cup thick whipped cream
- 2 teaspoons bell pepper
- 1 tablespoon white sugar
- 1 tablespoon vegetable oil
- 4 boneless and skinless chicken fillets, cut into small pieces
- 1 teaspoon salt
- ½ teaspoon of curry powder
- 1 teaspoon of white sugar

Instructions

1. Heat the ghee in a big frying pan over medium-high heat; cook and stir the onion until light, about 5 minutes. Stir in the garlic;

cook and stir until fragrant, about 1 minute. Stir the caraway, 1 teaspoon of salt, ginger, cayenne pepper, cinnamon, and turmeric into the onion mixture; bake until fragrant, about 2 minutes.

2. Stir the tomato sauce into the onion-herb mixture, bring to a boil and reduce the heat. Let the sauce simmer for 10 minutes and stir in the cream, bell pepper, and 1 tablespoon sugar. Let the sauce simmer and cook, stirring until the sauce thickens, 10 to 15 minutes.

3. Heat the vegetable oil in a different frying pan over medium heat. Stir the chicken in hot oil, sprinkle with curry powder, and sear the chicken light brown but still pink on the inside, about 3 minutes, stirring often. Transfer the chicken and the gravy to the sauce. Wait for the chicken simmer in the sauce until it is no longer pink, about 30 minutes; adjust the salt and sugar to taste.

Macros
Per serving: 328 calories; 23.4 grams of total fat; 106 mg of cholesterol; 980 mg of sodium. 13.2 g carbohydrates; 17.9 g of protein

47. Caramel Popcorn

Prep time: 30 minutes
Servings: 20

Ingredients
- 1 cup butter
- 2 cups brown sugar
- 1/2 cup of corn syrup
- 1 teaspoon salt
- 1/2 teaspoon baking powder
- 1 teaspoon vanilla extract
- 5 cups of popcorn

Instructions
1. Preheat the oven to 95° C (250° F). Put the popcorn in a large bowl.
2. Melt the butter in a medium-sized pan over medium heat. Stir in brown sugar, salt, and corn syrup. Bring to a boil, constantly stirring — Cook without stirring for 4 minutes. Then remove from heat and stir in the soda and vanilla. Pour in a thin layer on the popcorn and stir well.
3. Place in two large shallow baking tins and bake in the preheated oven, stirring every 15

minutes for an hour. Remove from the oven and let cool completely before breaking into pieces.

Macros
Per serving: 14 g fat; 253 calories; 32.8 g carbohydrates; 0.9 g of protein; 24 mg cholesterol; 340 mg of sodium

48. Tiramisu

Prep time: 30 minutes
Servings: 12

Ingredients
- 6 egg yolks
- 3/4 cup white sugar
- 2/3 cup milk
- 1 1/4 cup whipped cream
- 1/2 teaspoon vanilla extract
- 1 pound of mascarpone
- 1/4 cup of strong coffee, room temperature
- 2 tablespoons rum
- 2 (3-gram) ladyfinger cookie packages
- 1 tablespoon unsweetened cocoa powder

Instructions
1. In a medium saucepan, beat egg yolks and sugar well. Beat in milk and cook over medium heat, constantly stirring until the mixture boils. Cook gently for 1 minute, remove from heat and let cool slightly. Cover and let cool in the fridge for 1 hour.
2. In a medium bowl, beat the vanilla cream until stiff peaks form. Beat the mascarpone in the yellow mixture until a smooth texture is obtained.
3. Mix the coffee and the rum in a small bowl. Divide the ladyfingers in half and sprinkle with the coffee mixture.
4. Place half of the soaked fingers on the bottom of a 7 x 11-inch dish. Spread half of the mascarpone mixture over the ladyfingers and then half of the whipped cream. Repeat the layers and sprinkle with cocoa. Cover and leave it in the fridge for 4 to 6 hours before to serve

Macros
Per serving: 387 calories 30.5 g fat; 22.7 g of carbohydrates; 6.6 g of protein; 216 mg of cholesterol; 60 mg of sodium

49. White Chocolate Raspberry Cheesecake

Prep time: 1 hour
Servings: 16
Ingredients

- 1 cup chocolate cookie breadcrumbs
- 3 tablespoons white sugar
- 1/4 cup melted butter
- 1 packet of frozen raspberries
- 10 tablespoons of white sugar
- 2 teaspoons of corn flour
- 1/2 cup of water
- 2 cups of white chocolate chips
- 1/2 cup half and half cream
- 3 (8-gram) packages of cream cheese, softened
- 1/2 cup white sugar
- 3 eggs
- 1 teaspoon vanilla extract

Instructions

1. Combine breadcrumbs, 3 tablespoons sugar, and melted butter in a medium bowl. Squeeze the mixture into the bottom of a 9-inch hinged pan.
2. Combine raspberries, 2 tablespoons sugar, corn flour and water in a pan. Now bring to a boil and continue to cook for 5 minutes or until the sauce is thick. Filter the sauce through a colander to remove the seeds.
3. Preheat the oven to 165° C (325° F). Melt the white chocolate chips in a metal bowl in a pan with boiling water, occasionally stirring, until a smooth mixture.
4. Combine cream cheese and 1/2 cup of sugar in a large bowl until smooth. Beat the eggs one by one. Stir vanilla and melted white chocolate. Pour half of the dough over the crust. Pour 3 tablespoons of raspberry sauce over the dough. Pour the rest of the cheese batter into the frying pan and pour over 3 tablespoons of raspberry sauce. Turn the dough with the tip of a knife to create a marble effect.
5. Bake for 55 to 60 minutes then leave to cool before placing it in the fridge for 8 hours.
6. Remove it from the pan and serve with the left over raspberry sauce.

Macros
Per serving: 412 calories; 28.3 g of fat; 34.4 g carbohydrates; 6.8 g of protein; 96 mg cholesterol; 226 mg of sodium.

50. Double Tomato Bruschetta

Prep time: 15 minutes
Servings: 12
Ingredients

- 6 Roma tomatoes, diced
- 1/2 cup of sun-dried tomatoes in oil
- 3 cloves of chopped garlic
- 1/4 cup of olive oil
- 1/4 cup fresh basil, stems removed
- 2 tablespoons balsamic vinegar
- 1/4 teaspoon salt
- 1/4 teaspoon ground black pepper
- 1 French baguette
- 2 cups of grated mozzarella cheese

Instruction

1. Preheat the oven to the grill setting.
2. Mix Roma tomatoes, sun dried tomatoes, garlic, olive oil, vinegar, basil, salt, and pepper in a large bowl. Let the mixture stand for 10 minutes.
3. Cut the baguette into 3/4 inch slices. Place the baguettes on a baking sheet in a single layer. Grill for 1 to 2 minutes, until light brown.
4. Spread the tomato mixture evenly over the baguettes. Cover with the mozzarella cheese slices.
5. Grill for 5 minutes or until cheese is melted.

Macros
Per serving: 215 calories; 8.9 grams of fat; 24.8 g carbohydrates; 9.6 g of protein; 12 mg cholesterol; 426 mg of sodium

51. Greek Baklava

Prep time: 30 minutes
Servings: 18
Ingredients

- 1 phyllo dough package (16 ounces)
- 1 pound of chopped walnuts
- 1 cup butter
- 1 teaspoon ground cinnamon
- 1 cup of water, 1 cup of white sugar
- 1 teaspoon vanilla extract
- 1/2 cup honey

Instructions

1. Preheat the oven to 175° C (350° F). Butter the bottom and sides of a 9 x 13-inch pan.
2. Chop the nuts and mix them with cinnamon. Set aside. Roll out the phyllo dough. Cut the whole stack in half to adapt to the pan. Cover phyllo with a damp cloth to prevent it from drying out while you work.
3. Place two sheets of dough in the pan, butter carefully. Repeat this until you have 8 overlapping sheets. Sprinkle 2 - 3 tablespoons of walnut mixture on top. Cover with two sheets of dough, butter, nuts, and layers as you go. The top layer must have a depth of around 6-8 leaves.
4. Cut a diamond or square to the bottom of the pan with a sharp knife. You can cut the diagonal cuts into 4 long rows. Bake for about 50 minutes until the baklava is golden brown and crispy.
5. Make the sauce while the baklava is cooking. Boil the sugar and water until the sugar has melted. Add vanilla and honey. Let simmer for about 20 minutes.
6. Remove the baklava from the oven and immediately pour the sauce over it. Let cool. Serve in a cupcake paper.

Macros

Per serving: 393 calories; 25.9 g fat; 37.5 g carbohydrates; 6.1 g of protein; 27 mg cholesterol; 196 mg of sodium.

52. Catherine's Spicy Chicken Soup

Prep time: 15 minutes
Servings: 8
Ingredients
- 2 liters of water
- 8 half chicken breasts without skin and without bone
- ½ teaspoon of salt
- 1 teaspoon ground black pepper
- 1 teaspoon garlic powder
- 2 tablespoons dried parsley
- 1 tablespoon onion powder
- 5 cubes of chicken broth
- 3 tablespoons of olive oil
- 1 onion, minced
- 3 garlic cloves, minced
- 1 large jar of salsa (16 oz)
- 2 cans (14.5 oz) diced tomatoes
- 1 (14.5 oz) peeled whole tomatoes
- 1 (10.75 oz) condensed tomato soup
- 3 tablespoons chili powder
- 1 can of whole-grain corn
- 1 can of chili beans, undrained
- 8 oz of sour cream

Instructions

1. Mix water, chicken, salt, pepper, garlic powder, parsley, onion powder, and stock cubes in a large pan over medium heat. Bring to a boil, reduce the heat and simmer for 1 hour, or until the chicken juice is clear. Remove the chicken, save the broth. Shred the chicken.
2. Fry onion and garlic in olive oil in a large saucepan over medium heat until lightly browned. Stir in the salsa, tomato cubes, whole tomatoes, tomato soup, chili powder, corn, green beans, sour cream, grated chicken, and 5 cups of broth. Let simmer for 30 minutes.

Macros

Per serving: 473 calories 15.3 grams of total fat; 82 mg of cholesterol; 2436 mg of sodium. 50.3 g carbohydrates; 39.6 g of protein

53. Terrific Turkey Chili

Prep time: 15 minutes
Servings: 6
Ingredients
- 3 tablespoons vegetable oil
- 1 1/2 pound ground turkey
- 1 taco spice mix (1 oz)
- 1 teaspoon ground coriander
- 1 teaspoon dried oregano
- 1 teaspoon chili flakes
- 2 tablespoons tomato puree
- 1 can beef broth (14.5 oz)
- 1 can of salsa (7 oz)
- 1 can of crushed tomatoes (14.5 oz)
- 1 can of chopped green pepper
- 1 medium onion, finely chopped
- 1 green pepper, diced
- 3 medium-sized zucchini, halved lengthwise and sliced
- 1 bunch of green onions, minced
- 1 cup sour cream
- 1 cup grated cheddar cheese

Instruction

1. Heat 1 tablespoon of oil in a large saucepan over medium heat. Crumble the turkey in the pot by mixing it with a wooden spoon to separate as much as possible. Season with the taco-spice mix, coriander, oregano, chili flakes, and tomato puree and mix until the meat is seasonally covered with herbs. Keep cooking, reduce the heat if necessary, until the turkey is golden brown.

2. Pour the beef broth and simmer to reduce the liquid slightly, about 5 minutes. Add salsa, tomatoes, and bell peppers and cook for another 10 minutes on low heat. Adjust the thickness at any time by adding water.

3. Heat a tablespoon of oil in a large frying pan over medium-high heat. Sauté the onion and green pepper, occasionally stirring for 5 minutes or until the onion is transparent, and the pepper is light brown. Add onion and chili pepper and cook over low heat.

4. In the same frying pan, heat the remaining spoon of oil over medium heat. Add the zucchini and cook for 5 minutes or until lightly browned. Add the zucchini to the chili, lower the heat and cook for another 15 minutes. Readjust consistency with water as needed.

5. Divide the chili into bowls. Garnish with sour cream, green onions, and cheddar cheese and serve.

Macros

Per serving: 506 calories; 31.9 g of fat; 24.1 g carbohydrates; 34.7 g of protein; 125 mg cholesterol; 1521 mg of sodium.

CHAPTER 3: SALADS

There are tons of salad recipes available. These salads are great because they are versatile. You can serve a potato salad as a side dish with many different main dishes such as with ribs, burgers, chicken salad, grilled chicken, baked chicken, and sandwiches. A variety of salads can be prepared in just a few minutes. Here are some quick salad recipes:

54. Cucumber Chicken Salad with Spicy Peanut Dressing

Prep time: 15 minutes

Servings: 2

Ingredients

- 1/2 cup peanut butter
- 1 tablespoon sambal oelek (chili paste)
- 1 tablespoon low-sodium soy sauce
- 1 teaspoon grilled sesame oil
- 4 tablespoons of water, or more if necessary
- 1 cucumber with peeled and cut into thin strips
- 1 cooked chicken fillet, grated into thin strips
- 2 tablespoons chopped peanuts

Instructions

1. Combine peanut butter, soy sauce, sesame oil, sambal oelek, and water in a bowl.
2. Place the cucumber slices on a dish. Garnish with grated chicken and sprinkle with sauce. Sprinkle the chopped peanuts.

Macros

Per serving: 54 g fat; 20.6 g 720 **calories**; **carbohydrates**; 45.9 g **protein**; 89 mg **cholesterol**; 789 mg of **sodium**.

55. German Hot Potato Salad

Prep time: 10 minutes

Servings: 12

Ingredients

- 9 peeled potatoes
- 6 slices of bacon
- 1/8 teaspoon ground black pepper
- 1/2 teaspoon celery seed
- 2 tablespoons white sugar
- 2 teaspoons salt
- 3/4 cup water
- 1/3 cup distilled white vinegar
- 2 tablespoons all-purpose flour
- 3/4 cup chopped onions

Instruction

1. Bring a large pot of salted water to a boil. Add the potatoes and cook until soft but still firm, about 30 minutes. Drain, let cool and cut finely.
2. Cook the bacon in a frying pan over medium heat. Drain, crumble and set aside. Save the cooking juices.
3. Fry onions in bacon grease until golden brown.
4. Combine flour, sugar, salt, celery seed, and pepper in a small bowl. Add sautéed onions and cook, stirring until bubbling, and remove from heat. Stir in the water and vinegar, then bring back to the fire and bring to a boil, stirring constantly. Boil and stir. Slowly add bacon and potato slices to the vinegar/water mixture, stirring gently until the potatoes are warmed up.

Macros

Per serving: 205 **calories**; 6.5 g of **fat**; 32.9 g **carbohydrates**; 4.3 g of **protein**; 10 mg **cholesterol**; 512 mg of **sodium**.

56. Chicken Fiesta Salad

Prep time: 40 minutes

Servings: 4

Ingredients

- 2 halves of chicken fillet without skin or bones
- 1 packet of herbs for fajitas, divided
- 1 tablespoon vegetable oil
- 1 can black beans, rinsed and drained
- 1 box of Mexican-style corn
- 1/2 cup of salsa
- 1 packet of green salad
- 1 onion, minced
- 1 tomato, quartered

Instructions

1. Rub the chicken evenly with 1/2 of the herbs for fajitas. Heat the oil in a frying pan over medium heat and cook the chicken for 8 minutes on the side by side or until the juice is clear; put aside.
2. Combine beans, corn, salsa, and other 1/2 fajita spices in a large pan. Heat over medium heat until lukewarm.
3. Prepare the salad by mixing green vegetables, onion, and tomato.
4. Cover the chicken salad and dress the beans and corn mixture.

Macros

Per serving: 311 **calories**; 6.4 g **fat**; 42.2 g **carbohydrates**; 23 g of **protein**; 36 mg of **cholesterol**; 1606 mg of **sodium**.

57. Corn & Black Bean Salad

Prep time: 10 minutes

Servings: 4

Ingredients

- 2 tablespoons vegetable oil
- 1/4 cup balsamic vinegar
- 1/2 teaspoon of salt
- 1/2 teaspoon of white sugar
- 1/2 teaspoon ground cumin
- 1/2 teaspoon ground black pepper
- 1/2 teaspoon chili powder
- 3 tablespoons chopped fresh coriander
- 1 can black beans (15 oz), rinsed and drained
- 1 can of sweetened corn (8.75 oz) drained

Instructions

1. Combine balsamic vinegar, oil, salt, sugar, black pepper, cumin and chili powder in a small bowl.
2. Combine black corn and beans in a medium bowl. Mix with vinegar and oil vinaigrette and garnish with coriander. Cover and refrigerate overnight.

Macros

Per serving: 214 **calories**; 8.4 g **fat**; 28.6 g **carbohydrates**; 7.5 g of **protein**; 0 mg of **cholesterol**; 805 mg of **sodium**.

58. Awesome Pasta Salad

Prep time: 40 minutes

Servings: 16

Ingredients

- 1 (16-oz) fusilli pasta package
- 3 cups of cherry tomatoes, cut in half
- 1/2 pound of provolone, diced
- 1/2 pound of sausage, diced
- 1/4 pound of pepperoni, cut in half
- 1 large green pepper, cut into 1-inch pieces, 1 can of black olives, drained
- 1 jar of chilis, drained
- 1 bottle (8 oz) Italian vinaigrette

Instructions

1. Boil lightly salted water in a large panAdd pasta and cook for about 8 to 10 minutes or until al dente. Drain and rinse with cold water.
2. Combine pasta with tomatoes, cheese, salami, pepperoni, green pepper, olives, and peppers in a large bowl. Pour the vinaigrette and mix well.

Macros

Per serving: 310 calories; 17.7 grams of fat; 25.9 g carbohydrates; 12.9 g of protein; 31 mg of cholesterol; 913 mg of sodium.

59. Tuna Salad

Prep time: 20 minutes

Servings: 4

Ingredients

- 1 (19 ounce) can of garbanzo beans (chickpeas), drained and pureed
- 2 tablespoons mayonnaise
- 2 teaspoons of spicy brown mustard
- 1 tablespoon sweet pickle
- Salt and pepper to taste
- 2 chopped green onions

Instructions

1. Combine green beans, mayonnaise, mustard, sauce, chopped green onions, salt and pepper in a medium bowl. Mix well.

Macros: Per serving: 220 calories; 7.2 g fat; 32.7 g carbohydrates; 7 g of protein; 3 mg of cholesterol; 507 mg of sodium

60. Southern Potato Salad

Prep time: 30 minutes

Servings: 4

Ingredients

- 4 potatoes
- 4 eggs
- 1/2 stalk of celery, finely chopped
- 1/4 cup sweet taste
- 1 clove of garlic minced
- 2 tablespoons mustard
- 1/2 cup mayonnaise
- salt and pepper to taste

Instructions

1. Bring a large pot of salted water to a boil. Add the potatoes and cook until soft but still firm, about 15 minutes; drain and chop.
2. Place the eggs in a pan and cover with cold water. Boil the water; cover, remove from heat, and let the eggs rest in hot water for 10 to 12 minutes. Remove from hot water; peel and chop.
3. Combine potatoes, eggs, celery, sweet sauce, garlic, mustard, mayonnaise, salt, and pepper in a large bowl. Mix and serve hot.

Macros

Per serving: 460 calories; 27.4 grams of fat; 44.6 g carbohydrates; 11.3 g of protein; 196 mg cholesterol; 455 mg of sodium.

61. Seven-Layer Salad

Prep time: 15 minutes

Servings: 10

Ingredients

- 1 pound bacon
- 1 head iceberg lettuce - rinsed, dried and minced
- 1 red onion, minced
- 1 pack of 10 frozen peas, thawed
- 10 oz grated cheddar cheese
- 1 cup chopped cauliflower
- 1 1/4 cup mayonnaise
- 2 tablespoons white sugar
- 2/3 cup grated Parmesan cheese

Instructions

1. Put the bacon in a big, deep frying pan. Bake over medium heat until smooth. Crumble and set aside.

2. Place the chopped lettuce in a large bowl and cover with a layer of an onion, peas, grated cheese, cauliflower, and bacon.
3. Prepare the vinaigrette by mixing the mayonnaise, sugar, and parmesan cheese. Pour over the salad and cool to cool.

Macros

Per serving: 387 calories 32.7 grams of fat; 9.9 g of carbohydrates; 14.5 g of protein; 51 mg of cholesterol; 667 mg of sodium.

62. Kale, Quinoa & Avocado Salad with Lemon Dijon Vinaigrette

Prep time: 25 minutes

Servings: 4

Ingredients

- 2/3 cup of quinoa, 1 1/3 cup of water
- 1 bunch of kale, torn into bite-sized pieces, 1/2 avocado - peeled, diced and pitted
- 1/2 cup chopped cucumber
- 1/3 cup chopped red pepper
- 2 tablespoons chopped red onion
- 1 tablespoon of feta crumbled

Instructions

1. Bring the quinoa and 1 1/3 cup of water to a boil in a pan. Reduce heat to low, cover, and simmer until quinoa is soft and water is absorbed for about 15 to 20 minutes. Set aside to cool.
2. Place the cabbage in a steam basket over more than an inch of boiling water in a pan. Cover the pan with a lid and steam until hot, about 45 seconds; transfer to a large plate. Garnish with cabbage, quinoa, avocado, cucumber, pepper, red onion, and feta cheese.
3. Combine olive oil, lemon juice, Dijon mustard, sea salt, and black pepper in a bowl until the oil is emulsified in the dressing; pour over the salad.

Macros

Per serving: 342 calories; 20.3 g of fat; 35.4 g carbohydrates; 8.9 g of protein; 2 mg of cholesterol; 552 mg of sodium.

63. Carol's Chicken Salad

Prep time: 20 minutes

Servings: 9

Ingredients

- 1/2 cup mayonnaise
- 1/2 teaspoon of salt
- 3/4 teaspoon of poultry herbs
- 1 tablespoon lemon juice
- 3 cups cooked chicken breast, diced
- 1/4 teaspoon ground black pepper
- 1/4 teaspoon garlic powder
- 1/4 teaspoon onion powder
- 1/2 cup finely chopped celery
- 1 (8 oz) box of water chestnuts, drained and chopped
- 1/2 cup chopped green onions
- 1 1/2 cups green grapes cut in half
- 1 1/2 cups diced Swiss cheese

Instructions

1. Combine mayonnaise, salt, chicken spices, onion powder, garlic powder, pepper, and lemon juice in a medium bowl.
2. Combine chicken, celery, green onions, water chestnuts, Swiss cheese, and raisins in a big bowl. Add the mayonnaise mixture and stir to coat. Cool until ready to serve.

Macros

Per serving: 293 calories; 19.5 grams of fat; 10.3 g carbohydrates; 19.4 g of protein; 60 mg cholesterol; 279 mg of sodium.

64. Cobb Salad

Prep time: 20 minutes

Servings: 6 servings

Ingredients

- 6 slices of bacon
- 3 eggs
- 1 cup Iceberg lettuce, grated
- 3 cups cooked minced chicken meat
- 2 tomatoes, seeded and minced
- 3/4 cup of blue cheese, crumbled
- 1 avocado - peeled, pitted and diced
- 3 green onions, minced
- 1 bottle (8 oz.) Ranch Vinaigrette

Instructions

1. Place the eggs in a pan and cover them completely with cold water. Boil the water. Cover and remove from heat and let the eggs rest in hot water for 10 to 12 minutes. Remove from hot water, let cool, peel, and chop.
2. Put the bacon in a big, deep frying pan. Bake over medium heat until smooth. Drain, crumble, and reserve.
3. Divide the grated lettuce into separate plates.
4. Spread chicken, eggs, tomatoes, blue cheese, bacon, avocado, and green onions in rows on lettuce.
5. Sprinkle with your favorite vinaigrette and enjoy.

Macros

Per serving: 525 calories; 39.9 g fat; 10.2 g carbohydrates; 31.7 g of protein; 179 mg cholesterol; 915 mg of sodium.

65. Alyson's Broccoli Salad

Prep time: 10 minutes

Servings: 6

Ingredients

- 10 slices of bacon
- 1 cup fresh broccoli, cut into small pieces
- ¼ cup red onion, minced
- ½ cup raisins
- 3 tablespoons white wine vinegar
- 2 tablespoons white sugar
- 1 cup mayonnaise
- 1 cup of sunflower seeds

Instructions

1. Cook the bacon in a deep frying pan over medium heat. Drain, crumble, and set aside.
2. Combine broccoli, onion, and raisins in a medium bowl. Mix vinegar, sugar, and mayonnaise in a small bowl. Pour over the broccoli mixture and mix. Cool for at least two hours.
3. Before serving, mix the salad with crumbled bacon and sunflower seeds.

Macros

Per serving: 559 calories 48.1 grams of total fat; 31 mg of cholesterol; 584 mg of sodium. 23.9 g carbohydrates; 12.9 g of protein

66. Strawberry Spinach Salad

Prep time: 10 minutes
Servings: 4
Ingredients

- 2 tablespoons sesame seeds
- 1 tablespoon poppy seeds
- 1/2 cup white sugar
- 1/2 cup olive oil
- 1/4 cup distilled white vinegar
- 1/4 teaspoon paprika
- 1/4 teaspoon Worcestershire sauce
- 1 tablespoon minced onion,
- 10 ounces fresh spinach - rinsed, dried and torn into bite-size pieces
- 1-quart strawberries - cleaned, hulled and sliced
- 1/4 cup almonds, blanched and slivered

Instructions

1. In a medium bowl, whisk together the same seeds, poppy seeds, sugar, olive oil, vinegar, paprika, Worcestershire sauce, and onion. Cover, and chill for one hour.
2. In a large bowl, combine the spinach, strawberries, and almonds. Pour dressing over salad and toss. Refrigerate 10 to 15 minutes before serving.

Macros

Per serving: 491 calories; 35.2 g fat; 42.9 g carbohydrates; 6 g protein; 0 mg cholesterol; 63 mg sodium

67. Pear Salad with Roquefort Cheese

Prep time: 20 minutes
Servings: 2
Ingredients

- 1 leaf lettuce, torn into bite-sized pieces
- 3 pears - peeled, cored and diced
- 5 ounces Roquefort, crumbled
- 1 avocado - peeled, seeded and diced
- 1/2 cup chopped green onions
- 1/4 cup white sugar
- 1/2 cup pecan nuts
- 1/3 cup olive oil
- 3 tablespoons red wine vinegar
- 1 1/2 teaspoon of white sugar
- 1 1/2 teaspoon of prepared mustard
- 1/2 teaspoon of salted black pepper
- 1 clove of garlic

Instructions

1. In a frying pan over medium heat, mix 1/4 cup of sugar with the pecans. Continue to stir gently until the sugar has melted and is caramelized with pecans. Carefully transfer the nuts to wax paper. Allow to cool and break into pieces.
2. Mix for vinaigrette oil, vinegar, 1 1/2 teaspoon of sugar, mustard, chopped garlic, salt, and pepper.
3. In a large bowl, add lettuce, pears, blue cheese, avocado, and green onions. Pour vinaigrette over salad, sprinkle with pecans and serve.

Macros

Per serving: 426 calories; 31.6 g fat; 33.1 g carbohydrates; 8 g of protein; 21 mg of cholesterol; 654 mg of sodium.

68. Mexican Bean Salad

Prep time: 15 minutes
Servings: 6
Ingredients

- 1 can black beans (15 oz), drained
- 1 can red beans (15 oz), drained
- 1 can white beans (15 oz), drained
- 1 green pepper, minced
- 1 red pepper, minced
- 1 pack of frozen corn kernels
- 1 red onion, minced
- 2 tablespoons fresh lime juice
- 1/2 cup olive oil
- 1/2 cup red wine vinegar
- 1 tablespoon lemon juice
- 1 tablespoon salt
- 2 tablespoons white sugar
- 1 clove of crushed garlic
- 1/4 cup chopped coriander
- 1/2 tablespoon ground cumin
- 1/2 tablespoon ground black pepper
- 1 dash of hot pepper sauce
- 1/2 teaspoon chili powder

Instructions

1. Combine beans, peppers, frozen corn, and red onion in a large bowl.
2. Combine olive oil, lime juice, red wine vinegar, lemon juice, sugar, salt, garlic, coriander, cumin, and black pepper in a

small bowl — season with hot sauce and chili powder.

3. Pour the vinaigrette with olive oil over the vegetables; mix well. Cool well and serve cold.

Macros

Per serving: 334 calories; 14.8 g of fat; 41.7 g of carbohydrates; 11.2 g of protein; 0 mg of cholesterol; 1159 mg of sodium.

69. Jamie's Cranberry Spinach Salad

Prep time: 10 minutes
Servings: 6
Ingredients
- 1 tablespoon butter
- 3/4 cup almonds, blanched and cut into pieces
- 1 pound of spinach, rinsed and torn into bite-sized pieces
- 1 cup dried cranberries
- 2 tablespoons roasted sesame seeds
- 1 tablespoon poppy seeds
- 1/2 cup white sugar
- 2 teaspoons chopped onion
- 1/4 teaspoon bell pepper
- 1/4 cup white wine vinegar
- 1/4 cup cider vinegar
- 1/2 cup vegetable oil

Instructions
1. Melt the butter in a medium-sized pan over medium heat. Cook and add the almonds to the butter until lightly roasted. Remove from heat and let cool.
2. Combine the sesame seeds, poppy seeds, sugar, onion, bell pepper, white wine vinegar, apple cider vinegar, and vegetable oil in a medium bowl. Mix the spinach just before serving.
3. In a large bowl, mix spinach with roasted almonds and cranberries.

Macros

Per serving: 338 calories; 23.5 grams of fat; 30.4 g carbohydrates; 4.9 g of protein; 4 mg cholesterol; 58 mg of sodium.

70. Zesty Quinoa Salad

Prep time: 20 minutes
Servings: 6
Ingredients

- 2 limes, juiced
- 2 teaspoons cumin powder
- 1 teaspoon salt
- 1 cup quinoa
- 2 cups water
- 1/4 cup extra virgin olive oil
- 1/2 teaspoon red pepper flakes
- 1 1/2 cup cherry tomatoes cut in half
- 1 can black beans (15 oz), drained and rinsed
- 5 green onions, finely chopped
- 1/4 cup chopped fresh coriander
- ground black pepper to taste

Instructions
1. Bring the quinoa and water to a boil in a pan. Reduce heat to low, cover, and simmer until quinoa is soft and water is absorbed for 10 to 15 minutes. Set aside to cool.
2. Combine olive oil, lime juice, cumin, 1 teaspoon of salt, and red pepper flakes in a bowl.
3. Mix quinoa, tomatoes, black beans, and green onions in a bowl. Pour the vinaigrette over the quinoa mixture; mix to coat. Stir in the coriander; season with salt and black pepper. Serve immediately or keep in the refrigerator.

Macros

Per serving: 270 calories; 11.5 g of fat; 33.8 g carbohydrates; 8.9 g of protein; 0 mg of cholesterol; 675 mg of sodium.

71. Lamb's Lettuce

Prep time: 10 minutes
Servings: 4
Ingredients
- 8 grams of green salad
- 3/4 cup chopped walnuts
- 8 grams of crumbled gorgonzola
- 2 sharp green apples, hollowed out and diced
- 1/2 bottle of raspberry vinaigrette

Instructions
1. In a large bowl, mix salad vegetables, nuts, cheese, and apples. Mix with the raspberry vinaigrette and serve.

Macros

Per serving: 416 calories; 30.4 g of fat; 21.5 g carbohydrates; 16.4 g of protein; 60 mg cholesterol; 913 mg of sodium.

CHAPTER 4: RICE & GRAINS

Rice and grains have been cultivated for more than 5,000 years. With more than 7,000 varieties, rice has become the staple food of more than 50 percent of the world's population.

Asian countries produce around 90% of the world's rice, and Asian people consume up to 300 pounds of rice per person per year. Americans consume just over 21 kilos of rice per person per year, and the French consume around 10 kilos of rice per person per year.

Listed below are some delicious and fun whole rice and grain recipes that are easy to prepare and require minimal cooking time.

72. Long-Grain Rice Congee & Vietnamese Chicken

Prep time: 10 minutes
Servings: 4
Ingredients

- 1/8 cup uncooked jasmine rice
- 1 whole chicken (2.5 lb.)
- 3 pieces of fresh ginger root
- 1 stalk of lemongrass
- 1 tablespoon of salt
- 1/4 cup chopped coriander
- 1/8 cup chopped fresh chives
- ground black pepper to taste
- 1 lime, cut into 8 quarters

Instructions

1. Place the chicken in a pan. Pour enough water to cover the chicken. Add ginger, lemongrass, and salt; bring to a boil. Lower the heat, cover and let it simmer for 1 hour to an hour and a half.
2. Filter the broth and put the broth back in a pan. Allow the chicken to cool, then remove the bones and skin and tear into small pieces; put aside.
3. Add the rice to the broth and bring to a boil. Turn the heat to medium and cook for 30 minutes, stirring occasionally. Adjust if necessary with extra water or salt. The congee is done, but you can still cook for 45 minutes for better consistency.
4. Pour the congee into bowls and garnish with chicken, coriander, chives, and pepper. Squeeze the lime juice to taste.

Macros

Per serving: 642 calories; 42.3 g fat; 9.8 g of carbohydrates; 53 g of protein; 210 mg cholesterol; 1943 mg of sodium

73. Wild Rice Soup & Creamy Chicken

Prep time: 5 minutes
Servings: 8
Ingredients

- 4 cups of chicken broth
- 2 cups of water
- 2 half-cooked and boneless chicken breast, grated
- 1 pack (4.5 ounces) of long-grain fast-cooking rice with a spice pack
- 1/2 teaspoon of salt
- 1/2 teaspoon of ground black pepper
- 3/4 cup flour
- 1/2 cup butter
- 2 cups thick cream

Instructions

1. Combine broth, water, and chicken in a large saucepan over medium heat. Bring to a boil, stir in the rice, and save the seasoning package. Cover and remove from heat.
2. In a small bowl, mix the flour with salt and pepper. Using a medium-sized pan, melt some butter over medium heat. Stir the contents of the herb bag until the mixture bubbles. Reduce the heat and add the flour mixture to the tablespoon to form a roux. Stir the cream little by little until it is completely absorbed and smooth. Bake until thick, 5 minutes.
3. Add the cream mixture to the stock and rice — Cook over medium heat for 10 to 15 minutes.

Macros

Per serving: 462 calories; 36.5 grams of fat; 22.6 g carbohydrates; 12 g of protein; 135 mg cholesterol; 997 mg of sodium.

74. Best Spanish Rice

Prep time: 10 minutes

Servings: 5

Ingredients

- 2 tablespoons oil
- 2 tablespoons chopped onion
- 1 1/2 cups uncooked white rice
- 2 cups chicken broth
- 1 cup chunky salsa

Instructions

1. Heat the oil in a large frying pan over medium heat. Stir the onion and cook until tender, about 5 minutes.
2. Mix the rice in a pan, stirring often. When the rice starts to brown, stir in the chicken stock and salsa. Lower the heat, cover, and simmer for 20 minutes until liquid is absorbed.

Macros

Per serving: 286 calories; 6.2 g fat; 50.9 g carbohydrates; 5.7 g of protein; 2 mg of cholesterol; 697 mg of sodium.

75. Classic Rice Pilaf

Prep time: 10 minutes

Servings: 6

Ingredients

- 2 tablespoons butter
- 2 tablespoons olive oil
- 1/2 onion, minced
- 2 cups long-grain white rice
- 3 cups chicken broth
- 1 1/2 teaspoons of salt
- 1 pinch of saffron (optional)
- 1/4 teaspoon of cayenne pepper

Instructions

1. Bring the oven up to 175 ° C (350 ° F).
2. Heat the butter until it reaches liquid form.
3. Add melted butter and olive oil in a large saucepan over medium heat.
4. Add and cook minced onion, continuously stirring until the onion is light brown in colour, 7 to 8 minutes. Remove from the heat.
5. Combine rice and onion in a 9 x 13-inch baking dish on a baking sheet. Mix well to cover the rice.

6. Mix chicken broth, salt, saffron, and cayenne pepper in a pan. Bring to a boil, reduce the heat and simmer for 5 minutes.
7. Pour the chicken stock mixture over the rice in the casserole and mix. Spread the mixture evenly over the bottom of the pan. Cover firmly with sturdy aluminum foil.
8. Bake in the preheated oven for 35 minutes. Remove from the oven and leave under cover for 10 minutes. Remove the aluminum foil and stir with a fork to separate the rice grains.

Macros

Per serving: 312 calories; 9.1 g of fat; 51.7 g of carbohydrates; 5 g of protein; 11 mg cholesterol; 956 mg of sodium

76. Sarah's Rice Pilaf

Prep time: 10 minutes

Servings: 4 servings

Ingredients

- 2 tablespoons butter
- 1/2 cup orzo
- 1/2 cup diced onion
- 2 cloves finely chopped garlic
- 1/2 cup uncooked white rice
- 2 cups of chicken broth

Instructions

1. Melt the butter in a frying pan with a lid on medium heat. Boil and mix the orzo pasta golden brown.
2. Stir in the onion and cook until it is transparent, then add the garlic and cook for 1 minute.
3. Stir in the rice and chicken broth. Turn up the heat and bring to a boil. Lower the heat to medium, cover, and simmer until the rice is soft and the liquid is absorbed for 20 to 25 minutes. Remove from heat and let stand for 5 minutes, then stir with a fork.

Macros

Per serving: 244 calories; 6.5 g of fat; 40 g carbohydrates; 5.9 g of protein; 18 mg cholesterol; 524 mg of sodium.

77. Homemade Fried Rice

Prep time: 10 minutes
Servings: 8

Ingredients

- 1 1/2 cup uncooked white rice
- 3 tablespoons sesame oil
- 1 small onion, minced
- 1 clove of garlic, minced
- 1 cup peeled shrimp
- 1/2 cup diced ham
- 1 cup chopped cooked chicken fillet
- 2 celery stalks, minced
- 2 carrots, peeled and diced
- 1 green pepper, minced
- 1/2 cup of green peas
- 1 beaten egg
- 1/4 cup soy sauce

Instructions

1. Cook the rice according to the instructions on the package.
2. While cooking rice, heat a wok or large frying pan over medium heat. Pour in the sesame oil and sauté in the onion until golden brown. Add the garlic, shrimp, ham, and chicken. Cook until the shrimp are pink.
3. Reduce the heat and stir in celery, carrot, green pepper, and peas. Bake until the vegetables are soft. Stir in the beaten egg and cook until the egg is scrambled and firm.
4. When the rice is cooked, mix it with the vegetables and soy sauce.

Macros

Per serving: 236 calories; 8.4 g fat; 26.4 g carbohydrates; 13 g of protein; 59 mg cholesterol; 603 mg of sodium

78. Cranberry Rice

Prep time: 5 minutes
Servings: 6

Ingredients

- 2/3 cup uncooked brown rice
- 1 1/2 cups water
- 2 tablespoons canned cranberry sauce
- 1/2 cup of dried cranberries
- salt and black pepper to taste
- 1/4 cup chopped pecans

Instructions

1. Bring the brown rice and 1 1/2 cups of water to a boil in a pan over high heat. Reduce heat to low, cover, and simmer until the rice is soft and almost all of the liquid has been absorbed for 45 to 50 minutes.
2. Squash the cranberry sauce in a small bowl with a fork and mix with the brown rice. Cover and let steam for about 5 minutes.
3. Put the dried cranberries in a bowl microwave and cook them on high heat in the microwave for about 30 seconds. Stir the cranberries into the rice. Season with salt and black pepper; sprinkle with pecans.

Macros

Per serving: 129 calories; 3.7 g of fat; 23.4 grams of carbohydrates; 1.6 g of protein; 0 mg of cholesterol; 4 mg of sodium.

78. Kickin' Rice

Prep time: 10 minutes
Servings: 6

Ingredients

- 1 tablespoon of vegetable oil
- 1 cup of long-grain white rice
- 1 can of chopped green peppers
- 1 teaspoon of ground black pepper
- 2 cups of chicken broth

Instructions

1. Heat the vegetable oil in a pan over medium heat. Stir the rice in hot oil.
2. Add the green peppers and keep cooking until the rice starts to turn a little brown, 2 to 3 minutes.
3. Season the rice with pepper. Pour the stock into the pan; bring to a boil.
4. Reduce the heat to low, cover the pan and cook until the broth has been absorbed and the rice is soft, about 20 minutes.

Macros

Per serving: 83 calories; 2.6 g fat; 13 grams of carbohydrates 1.9 g of protein; 2 mg of cholesterol; 757 mg of sodium.

80. Garlic Rice

Prep time: 5 minutes

Servings: 4

Ingredients

- 2 tablespoons vegetable oil
- 1 1/2 tablespoons chopped garlic
- 2 tablespoons ground pork
- 4 cups cooked white rice
- 1 1/2 teaspoons of garlic salt
- ground black pepper to taste

Instructions

1. Heat the oil in a large frying pan over medium heat. When the oil is hot, add the garlic and ground pork. Boil and stir until garlic is golden brown.
2. Stir in cooked white rice and season with garlic salt and pepper. Bake and stir until the mixture is hot and well mixed for about 3 minutes.

Macros

Per serving: 293 calories; 9 g fat; 45.9 g carbohydrates; 5.9 g of protein; 6 mg cholesterol; 686 mg of sodium

81. Sweet Rice

Prep time: 10 minutes

Servings: 6

Ingredients

- 1 cup uncooked long-grain white rice
- 2 tablespoons unsalted butter
- 2 cups of water
- 2 cups of whole milk
- 1 tablespoon of all-purpose flour
- 1/3 cup white sugar
- 1 egg
- 1 1/2 teaspoon vanilla extract
- 1 cup whole milk
- 2/3 cup thick cream
- 1/2 cup raisins (optional)
- 1/2 teaspoon ground cinnamon

Instructions

1. Add rice and butter to water in a large saucepan and bring to boil over high heat. Once it begins to bubble, lower the heat to medium, cover, and simmer until the rice is soft and the liquid is absorbed for 20 to 25 minutes.
2. Mix 2 cups of milk, flour, sugar, egg, and vanilla extract in a bowl and pour the milk mixture over the cooked rice. Mix and simmer for 15 minutes over low heat.
3. Stir in 1 cup of whole milk, cream, raisins, and cinnamon until it is well mixed and let it cool for a few minutes.

Macros

Per serving: 418 **calories**; 18.7 **grams** of **fat**; 54.3 g **carbohydrates**; 8.6 g of **protein**; 90 mg of **cholesterol**; 76 mg of **sodium**.

82. Gourmet Mushroom Risotto

Prep time: 20 minutes

Servings: 6

Ingredients

- 1 kg Portobello mushrooms, minced,
- 1 pound of white mushrooms, minced
- 2 shallots, diced
- 3 tablespoons olive oil, divided
- 1 1/2 cup Arborio rice
- Salt and black pepper to taste
- 1/2 cup dry white wine
- 4 tablespoons butter
- 3 tablespoons finely chopped chives
- 6 cups chicken broth, divided
- 1/3 cup of freshly grated Parmesan cheese

Instructions

1. Heat the broth in a saucepan over low heat.
2. Heat 2 tablespoons of olive oil in a huge saucepan over medium heat. Stir in the mushrooms and cook until soft, about 3 minutes. Now remove the mushrooms and their liquid and set aside.
3. Put 1 tablespoon of olive oil in the pan and stir in the shallots. Cook for 1 minute and add the rice, stirring, to cover with oil for about 2 minutes. When the rice has turned a pale golden color, pour the wine constantly, stirring until the wine is completely absorbed.
4. Add 1/2 cup of rice broth and mix until the broth has been absorbed. Continue to add 1/2 cup of broth at a time, constantly stirring, until the liquid is absorbed and the rice is al dente, about 15 to 20 minutes.
5. Then remove from the heat and stir in the mushrooms with their liquid, butter, chives,

and Parmesan cheese. Season with salt and pepper.

Macros

Per serving: 431 calories; 16.6 g fat; 56.6 g carbohydrates; 11.3 g of protein; 29 mg of cholesterol; 1131 mg of sodium.

83. John's Beans and Rice

Prep time: 20 minutes
Servings: 8
Ingredients

- 1 lb. dry red beans
- 1 tablespoon of vegetable oil
- 12 grams of andouille sausage, diced
- 1 cup finely chopped onion
- 3/4 cup chopped celery
- 3/4 cup poblano peppers
- 4 cloves of garlic, minced
- 2 pints of chicken broth or more if necessary
- 1 smoked ham shank
- 2 bay leaves
- 1 teaspoon dried thyme
- 1/2 teaspoon cayenne pepper
- 1 teaspoon freshly ground black pepper
- 2 tablespoons chopped green onion,
- 4 cups cooked white rice

Instructions

1. Place the beans in a large container and cover them with a few centimeters of cold water; soak overnight. Drain and rinse.
2. Heat the vegetable oil in a large saucepan over medium heat. Cook and stir sausage in hot oil for 5 to 7 minutes. Stir in onion, celery, and poblano pepper in sausage; cook and stir until the vegetables soften and start to become transparent, 5 to 10 minutes. Add the garlic to the sausage mixture; cook and stir until fragrant, about 1 minute.
3. Stir in brown beans, chicken broth, ham shank, bay leaf, black pepper, thyme, cayenne pepper, and sausage mixture; bring to a boil, reduce the heat and stir occasionally, for an hour and a half.
4. Season with salt and simmer until the beans are soft, the meat is soft, and the desired consistency is achieved, 1 1/2 to 2 hours more. Season with salt.
5. Put the rice in bowls, place the red bean mixture on the rice and garnish with green onions.

Macros

Per serving: 542 calories; 20.5 grams of fat; 62.9 g carbohydrates; 25.9 g of protein; 46 mg cholesterol; 1384 mg of sodium.

84. Creamy Chicken & Wild Rice Soup

Prep time: 10 minutes
Servings: 8
Ingredients

- 2 cups of water
- 4 cups chicken broth
- 2 boneless chicken fillet and cooked, grated
- 1 pack (4.5 oz) long-grain fast-cooking rice with a spice pack
- ½ teaspoon of salt
- ½ teaspoon of ground black pepper
- ¾ cup of all-purpose flour
- ½ cup of butter
- 2 cups thick cream

Instructions

1. Combine broth, water, and chicken in a large saucepan over medium heat. Bring to a boil, stir in the rice, and save the seasoning package. Cover and remove from heat.
2. Combine salt, pepper, and flour in a small bowl. Melt the butter in a medium-sized pan over medium heat. Stir the contents of the herb bag until the mixture bubbles. Reduce the heat and add the flour mixture to the tablespoon to form a roux. Stir the cream little by little until it is completely absorbed and smooth. Bake until thick, 5 minutes.
3. Add the cream mixture to the stock and rice. Cook over medium heat for 10 to 15 minutes.

Macros

Per serving: 462 calories; 36.5 g total fat; 135 mg cholesterol; 997 mg of sodium. 22.6 g carbohydrates; 12 g of protein;

85. Carrot Rice

Prep time: 5 minutes
Servings: 6
Ingredients
- 2 cups of water
- 1 cube chicken broth
- 1 grated carrot
- 1 cup uncooked long-grain rice

Instructions
1. Bring the water to a boil in a medium-sized saucepan over medium heat. Place in the bouillon cube and let it dissolve.
2. Stir in the carrots and rice and bring to a boil again.
3. Lower the heat, cover, and simmer for 20 minutes.
4. Remove from heat and leave under cover for 5 minutes.

Macros
Per serving: 125 calories; 0.3 g of fat; 27.1 g carbohydrates; 2.7 g of protein; <1 mg cholesterol; 199 mg of sodium.

86. Rice Sauce

Prep time: 15 minutes
Servings: 6
Ingredients
- 3 cups of cooked rice
- 1 1/4 cup grated Monterey Jack cheese, divided
- 1 cup canned or frozen corn
- 1/2 cup of milk
- 1/3 cup of sour cream
- 1/2 cup chopped green onions

Instructions
1. Bring the oven up to 175 ° C (350 ° F).
2. Combine rice, a cup of cheese, corn, milk, sour cream, and green onions in a medium-sized bowl. Put in a 1-liter baking dish and sprinkle the rest of the cheese over it.
3. Bake in the preheated oven for 25 to 30 minutes or until cheese is melted and the dish is hot.

Macros
Per serving: 253 calories; 10.7 g of fat; 29.7 g of carbohydrates; 9.8 g of protein; 28 mg cholesterol; 225 mg of sodium.

87. Brown Rice

Prep time: 5 minutes
Servings: 4
Ingredients
- 1 1/2 cup uncooked long-grain white rice
- 1 (14 grams) beef broth
- 1 condensed soup of French onions
- 1/4 cup melted butter
- 1 tablespoon Worcestershire sauce
- 1 tablespoon dried basil leaves

Instruction
1. Bring the oven up to 175 ° C (350 ° F).
2. In a 2-quarter oven dish, combine rice, broth, soup, butter, Worcestershire sauce, and basil.
3. Cook for 1 hour, stirring after 30 minutes.

Macros
Per serving: 425 calories; 13.5 grams of fat; 66.2 g carbohydrates; 8.8 g of protein; 33 mg cholesterol; 1091 mg of sodium

88. Rice Lasagna

Prep time: 20 minutes
Servings: 8
Ingredients
- 1 pound ground beef
- spaghetti sauce in 1 (26 oz) jars
- 3 cups cooked rice, cooled, 1/2 teaspoon garlic powder
- 2 eggs, lightly beaten, 3/4 cup grated Parmesan cheese, divided
- 2 1/4 cup grated mozzarella cheese
- 2 cups of cottage cheese

Instructions
1. Preheat the oven to 190 ° C.
2. Heat up a large frying pan over medium heat. Fry and stir the meat in a hot pan until golden brown and crumbly, 5 to 7 minutes; drain the fat and discard it. Add the spaghetti sauce and garlic powder.
3. Mix the rice, eggs, and 1/4 cup Parmesan cheese in a bowl. Mix 2 cups mozzarella, cottage cheese, and 1/4 cup Parmesan cheese in another bowl.
4. Spread half of the rice mixture in a 3-liter baking dish, followed by half of the cheese mixture and half of the meat sauce. Repeat the layers. Sprinkle 1/4 cup Parmesan cheese

and 1/4 cup mozzarella on the last layer of meat sauce.

5. Bake in the preheated oven until cheese has melted and the sauce is bubbling, 20 to 25 minutes.

Macros

Per serving: 461 calories; 20.3 g of fat; 35.3 g carbohydrates; 32 g of protein; 118 mg of cholesterol; 975 mg of sodium

89. Rice Milk

Prep time: 5 minutes
Servings: 4
Ingredients

- 4 cups cold water
- 1 cup cooked rice
- 1 teaspoon vanilla extract (optional)

Instruction

1. Combine water, cooked rice, and vanilla extract in a blender; blend until smooth, about 3 minutes.
2. Chill before serving.

Macros

Per serving: 54 calories; 0.1 g fat; 11.3 g carbohydrates; 1.1 g protein; 0 mg cholesterol; 8 mg sodium.

CHAPTER 5: PASTA

Pasta recipes are diverse, and people of all ages and ethnicities can enjoy them. Pasta recipes can be made using fresh noodles or dry noodles, depending on taste or time one has to prepare them. Even the pickiest eater can enjoy a nice plate of pasta

Here are some pasta recipes that are easy to prepare.

90. Pasta Fazool (Pasta e Fagioli)

Prep time: 10 minutes

Servings: 2

Ingredients

- 1 tablespoon of olive oil,
- 12 ounces of Italian sweet bulk sausage
- 1 celery stem, diced
- 1/2 yellow onion, chopped
- 3/4 cup dry macaroni
- 1/4 cup tomato puree
- 3 cups chicken broth or more if necessary, divided
- salt and freshly ground black pepper
- 1/4 teaspoon of ground red pepper flakes
- 1/4 teaspoon dried oregano
- 3 cups finely chopped chard
- 1 can cannellini (15 oz), drained
- 1/4 cup grated Parmigiano-Reggiano cheese

Instructions

1. Heat the oil in a frying pan over medium heat. Brown the sausage by cutting it into small pieces, about 5 minutes. Return the heat to medium. Add diced celery and chopped onion. Bake until the onions are transparent, 4 to 5 minutes. Add the dry pasta. Boil and stir for 2 minutes.
2. Stir the tomato puree until smooth, 2 to 3 minutes. Add 3 cups of broth. Turn up the heat and let it simmer.
3. Season with salt, black pepper, pepper flakes, and oregano.
4. Lower heat once soup comes to a boil, then let it simmer for about 5 minutes, often stirring. Check the consistency of the soup and add stock if necessary.
5. Place the chopped chard in a bowl. And soak with cold water to rinse the leaves; some grain will fall to the bottom of the bowl. Transfer the chard to a colander to drain briefly; add to the soup. Boil and stir until the leaves fade, 2 to 3 minutes.
6. Stir in the white beans; keep cooking, stir until the pasta is cooked, 4 or 5 minutes. Remove from heat and stir in the grated cheese. Serve garnished with grated cheese, if desired.

Macros

Per serving: 888 calories; 43.8 g of fat; 77.3 g carbohydrates; 43.8 g of protein; 84 mg of cholesterol; 4200 mg of sodium.

91. Pasta Orecchiette Pasta

Prep time: 15 minutes

Servings: 2

Ingredients

- 2 tablespoons olive oil
- 1/2 onion, salt, diced to taste
- 8 grams of spicy Italian sausage
- 3 1/2 cups low-sodium chicken broth, divided
- 1 1/4 cup orecchiette pasta
- 1/2 cup of arugula
- 1/4 cup finely grated Parmigiano-Reggiano cheese

Instructions

1. Heat the olive oil in a deep frying pan over medium heat. Cook and stir the onion with a pinch of salt in hot oil until the onion is soft and golden brown, 5 to 7 minutes. Stir the sausages with onions; cook and stir until the sausages are golden brown, 5 to 7 minutes.
2. Pour 1 1/2 cup chicken stock into the sausage mixture and bring to a boil. Add the pasta to the orecchiette; boil and mix the pasta in a warm broth, add the remaining broth when the liquid is absorbed until the pasta is well cooked, and most of the broth is absorbed, about 15 minutes.
3. Spread the pasta in bowls and sprinkle with Parmigiano-Reggiano cheese.

Macros

Per serving: 662 calories; 39.1 grams of fat; 46.2 g

carbohydrates; 31.2 g of protein; 60 mg cholesterol; 1360 mg of sodium.

92. Shrimp Scampi with Pasta

Prep time: 20 minutes
Servings: 6
Ingredients

- 1 pack of linguine (16 oz)
- 2 tablespoons butter
- 2 tablespoons extra virgin olive oil
- 2 chopped shallots
- 2 cloves of chopped garlic
- 1 pinch of red pepper flakes
- 1 pound of shrimp, peeled and thawed
- 1 pinch of kosher salt and freshly ground pepper
- 1/2 cup of dry white wine
- 1 lemon, juiced
- 2 tablespoons butter
- 2 tablespoons extra virgin olive oil
- 1/4 cup finely chopped fresh parsley leaves
- 1 teaspoon extra virgin olive oil

Instructions

1. Boil a large pot of salted water to a boil; Add linguine in boiling water for 6 to 8 minutes until soft. Drain.
2. Melt 2 tablespoons of butter in a large frying pan followed by 2 tablespoons of olive oil over medium-high heat. Lightly fry the shallots, garlic, and red pepper flakes in the hot butter and oil until the shallots are transparent, 3 to 4 minutes. Season the shrimp with kosher salt and black pepper; Add to the pan and cook until pink, occasionally stirring, 2 to 3 minutes. Remove the shrimp from the pan and keep them warm.
3. Pour the white wine and lemon juice into the pan and bring to a boil. Melt 2 tablespoons of butter in a pan, mix 2 tablespoons of olive oil and let it simmer. Mix the linguine, shrimp, and parsley in the butter mixture until everything is well covered; Season with salt and black pepper. Sprinkle with 1 teaspoon of olive oil to serve.

Macros

Per serving: 511 calories; 19.4 g of fat; 57.5 g carbohydrates; 21.9 g of protein; 135 mg cholesterol;

260 mg of sodium

93. Pasta Salad with Chicken Club

Prep time: 20 minutes
Servings: 6
Ingredients

- 8 oz corkscrew pasta
- 3/4 cup Italian dressing
- 1/4 cup mayonnaise
- 2 cups roasted chicken cooked and minced
- 12 slices of crispy cooked bacon, crumbled
- 1 cup diced Münster cheese
- 1 cup chopped celery
- 1 cup chopped green pepper
- 8 oz. Cherry tomatoes, halved
- 1 avocado - peeled, seeded and chopped

Instructions

1. Boil a lightly salted water in a large pan Boil the pasta, occasionally stirring until well-cooked but firm, 10 to 12 minutes. Drain and rinse with cold water.
2. Beat the Italian dressing and mayonnaise in a large bowl. Stir the pasta, chicken, bacon, Münster cheese, celery, green pepper, cherry tomatoes, and avocado through the vinaigrette until everything is well mixed.

Macros

Per serving: 485 calories; 30.1 g fat; 37.1 g carbohydrates; 19.2 g of protein; 48 mg cholesterol; 723 mg of sodium.

94. Sausage Pasta

Prep time: 15 minutes
Servings: 6
Ingredients

- 3/4 pound of pasta
- 1 tablespoon of olive oil
- Spicy Italian sausage of 1 pound
- 1 onion, minced
- 4 cloves of chopped garlic
- 1 canned chicken broth
- 1 teaspoon dried basil
- 1 can diced tomatoes
- 1 pack (10 oz) of frozen chopped spinach
- 1/2 cup of grated Parmesan cheese

Instructions

1. Boil lightly salted water in a large pot, then add pasta and cook until al dente; (8-10 minutes)
2. Drain and set aside.
3. Heat oil and sausage in a large skillet; cook until pink. Add the onion and garlic to the pan during the last 5 minutes of cooking. Add the stock, basil, and tomatoes with the liquid.
4. Simmer over medium heat for 5 minutes to reduce slightly. Add the chopped spinach; cover the pan and simmer over low heat until the spinach is soft.
5. Add the pasta to the pan and mix. Sprinkle with cheese and serve immediately.

Macros

Per serving: 423 calories; 19.3 grams of fat; 39 g carbohydrates; 22.3 g of protein; 89 mg cholesterol; 1077 mg of sodium.

95. Pomodoro Pasta

Prep time: 15 minutes

Servings: 4

Ingredients

- 1 pack of 16 angel hair pasta
- 1/4 cup of olive oil
- 1/2 onion, minced
- 4 cloves of chopped garlic
- 2 cups of Roma tomatoes, diced
- 2 tablespoons balsamic vinegar
- 1 low-sodium chicken broth
- ground red pepper
- freshly ground black pepper to taste
- 1/4 cup grated Parmesan cheese
- 2 tablespoons chopped fresh basil

Instruction

1. Boil lightly salted water in a large panAdd pasta and cook for 8 minutes or until al dente; drain.
2. Pour the olive oil in a large deep pan over high heat. Fry onions and garlic until light brown. Lower the heat to medium and add tomatoes, vinegar, and chicken stock; simmer for about 8 minutes.
3. Stir in the red pepper, black pepper, basil, and cooked pasta and mix well with the sauce. Simmer for about 5 minutes and serve garnished with grated cheese.

Macros

Per serving: 500 calories 18.3 g fat; 69.7 g of carbohydrates; 16.2 g of protein; 6 mg cholesterol; 350 mg of sodium.

96. Tomato Cream Sauce

Prep time: 5 minutes

Servings: 5

Ingredients

- 2 tablespoons olive oil
- 1 onion, diced, 1 clove of garlic
- 1 can diced Italian tomatoes, not drained
- 1 tablespoon dried basil leaves
- 3/4 teaspoon white sugar
- 1/4 teaspoon dried oregano
- 1/4 teaspoon salt
- 1/8 teaspoon ground black pepper
- 1/2 cup heavy cream
- 1 tablespoon butter

Instruction

1. Fry onion and garlic in olive oil over medium heat.
2. Add tomatoes, basil, sugar, oregano, salt and pepper. Bring to a boil and cook for another 5 minutes or until most of the liquid has evaporated.
3. Remove from the heat; Stir in whipped cream and butter. Reduce the heat and simmer for another 5 minutes.

Macros

Per serving: 182 calories; 16.6 g fat; 6.7 grams of carbohydrates; 1.7 g of protein; 39 mg cholesterol; 270 mg of sodium.

97. Fra Diavolo Pasta Sauce

Prep time: 20 minutes
Servings: 8

Ingredients

4. 4 tablespoons olive oil, divided
5. 6 cloves of garlic, crushed
6. 3 cups peeled whole tomatoes with liquid, chopped
7. 1 1/2 teaspoon of salt
8. 1 teaspoon crushed red pepper flakes
9. 1 packet of linguine pasta
10. 8 grams of small shrimp, peeled
11. 8 grams of bay scallops
12. 1 tablespoon of chopped fresh parsley

Instructions

1. Heat 2 tablespoons of olive oil and sauté garlic over medium heat. When the garlic starts to sizzle, pour in the tomatoes. Season with salt and red pepper. Bring to boil. Reduce the heat and simmer for 30 minutes, stirring occasionally.
2. Meanwhile, boil a large pan with lightly salted water. Cook pasta for about 8 to 10 minutes or until al dente; drain.
3. Heat the remaining 2 tablespoons of olive oil in a large frying pan over high heat. Add shrimps and scallops. Cook for about 2 minutes stirring regularly, or until the shrimp turn pink. Add the shrimp and scallops to the tomato mixture and stir in the parsley. Bake for 3 to 4 minutes or until the sauce starts to bubble. Serve the sauce on the pasta.

Macros

Per serving: 335 calories; 8.9 grams of fat; 46.3 g carbohydrates; 18.7 g of protein; 52 mg of cholesterol; 655 mg of sodium.

98. Ranch Bacon Pasta Salad

Prep time: 10 minutes
Servings: 10

Ingredients

- 1 (12 oz.) package of uncooked tri color rotini
- 10 slices of bacon
- 1 cup mayonnaise
- 3 tablespoons dry ranch dressing powder
- 1/4 teaspoon of garlic powder
- 1/2 teaspoon of garlic pepper
- 1/2 cup of milk
- 1 large tomato, minced
- 1 can of sliced black olives (4.25 oz)
- 1 cup grated cheddar cheese

Instructions

1. Bring a large pot of lightly salted water to a boil; cook the rotini until tender but firm, about 8 minutes; drain.
2. Place the bacon in a frying pan over medium heat and cook until evenly browned. Drain and chop.
3. Combine mayonnaise, ranch dressing, garlic powder, and garlic pepper in a large bowl. Stir the milk until smooth.
4. Put the rotini, bacon, tomatoes, black olives, and cheese in a bowl and mix to cover with vinaigrette. Cover and put in the fridge for at least 1 hour.

Macros

Per serving: 336 calories; 26.8 g of fat; 14.9 g of carbohydrates; 9.3 g of protein; 31 mg of cholesterol; 691 mg of sodium. Complete food; 50 mg cholesterol; 1145 mg of sodium.

99. Alfredo Peppered Shrimp

Prep time: 20 minutes
Servings: 6

Ingredients

- 12 kg penne
- 1/4 cup butter
- 2 tablespoons extra virgin olive oil
- 1 onion, diced
- 2 cloves of chopped garlic
- 1 red pepper, diced
- 1/2 kg portobello mushrooms, cubed
- 1 pound shrimp, peeled and thawed
- 1 jar of Alfredo sauce
- 1/2 cup of grated Romano cheese
- 1/2 cup of cream
- 1/4 cup chopped parsley
- 1 teaspoon cayenne pepper
- salt and pepper to taste

Instructions

1. Boil lightly salted water in a large panPut the pasta and cook for 8 to 10 minutes or until al dente; drain.

2. Meanwhile, melt the butter and olive oil in a pan over medium heat. Stir in the onion and cook until soft and translucent, about 2 minutes. Stir in garlic, red pepper and mushrooms; cook over medium heat until soft, about 2 minutes longer.

3. Stir in the shrimp and fry until firm and pink, then add Alfredo sauce, Romano cheese and cream; bring to a boil, constantly stirring until thick, about 5 minutes. Season with cayenne pepper, salt, and pepper to taste. Add the drained pasta to the sauce and sprinkle with chopped parsley.

Macros

Per serving: 707 calories; 45 g fat; 50.6 g carbohydrates; 28.4 g of protein; 201 mg of cholesterol; 1034 mg of sodium.

100. Bow Ties with Sausages, Tomatoes & Cream

Prep time: 15 minutes
Servings: 6
Ingredients

- 1 package of bowtie pasta
- 2 tablespoons of olive oil
- 1 pound of sweet Italian sausages, crumbled
- 1/2 teaspoon of red pepper flakes
- 1/2 cup diced onion
- 3 finely chopped garlic cloves
- 1 can of Italian tomatoes, drained and roughly chopped
- 1 1/2 cup whipped cream
- 1/2 teaspoon salt
- 3 tablespoons fresh parsley

Instruction

1. Boil lightly salted water in a large panCook the pasta for 8 to 10 minutes in boiling water or until al dente; drain.

2. Heat the oil in a deep frying pan over medium heat. Cook the sausages and chili flakes until the sausages are golden brown. Stir in onion and garlic and cook until the onion is soft. Stir in the tomatoes, cream, and salt. Simmer until thickened, 8 to 10 minutes.

3. Add the pasta cooked in the sauce and heat. Sprinkle with parsley.

Macros

Per serving: 656 calories; 42.1 grams of fat; 50.9 g carbohydrates; 20.1 g of protein; 111 mg of

cholesterol; 1088 mg of sodium.

101. Penne with Spicy Vodka Tomato Cream Sauce

Prep time: 10 minutes
Servings: 8
Ingredients

- 1 pound uncooked penne
- 1/4 cup extra virgin olive oil
- 4 cloves finely chopped garlic
- 1/2 teaspoon crushed red pepper flakes
- 1 can of crushed tomatoes
- 3/4 teaspoon of salt
- 2 tablespoons of vodka
- 1/2 cup thick whipped cream
- 1/4 cup chopped fresh parsley
- 2 (3.5 ounces) sweet Italian sausage links

Instructions

1. Boil a lightly salted water in a large pan Put the pasta and cook for 8 to 10 minutes or until al dente; drain.

2. Heat the oil in a large frying pan over medium heat. Remove the casing from the sausage and add it to the pan. Cook by browning the meat, add garlic and red pepper and cook, stirring until the garlic is golden brown.

3. Add tomatoes and salt; boil. Lower the heat and simmer for 15 minutes.

4. Add vodka and cream and bring to a boil. Reduce the heat and add the pasta, mix for 1 minute. Stir in the fresh parsley and serve!

Macros

Per serving: 435 calories; 18.4 g fat; 52.7 g carbohydrates; 13.3 g of protein; 29 mg of cholesterol; 544 mg of sodium

102. Pesto with Basil and Spinach

Prep time: 20 minutes
Servings: 24
Ingredients

- 1 1/2 cup small spinach leaves
- 3/4 cup fresh basil leaves
- 1/2 cup grilled pine nuts
- 1/2 cup grated Parmesan cheese
- 4 cloves of garlic, peeled and quartered
- 3/4 teaspoon of kosher salt
- 1/2 teaspoon freshly ground black pepper
- 1 tablespoon fresh lemon juice
- 1/2 teaspoon lemon zest

- 1/2 cup extra virgin olive oil

Instructions
1. Mix spinach, basil, pine nuts, Parmesan, garlic, salt, pepper, lemon juice, lemon zest, and 2 tablespoons of olive oil in a food processor until smooth.
2. Sprinkle the remaining olive oil into the mixture.

Macros
Per serving: 67 calories; 6.6 g fat; 0.8 g carbohydrates; 1.5 g of protein; 1 mg cholesterol; 87 mg of sodium.

103. Milanese Chicken

Prep time: 10 minutes
Servings: 4
Ingredients
- ½ cup of sun-dried tomatoes, minced
- 1 cup of chicken broth, divided
- 1 cup thick cream
- 1 pound skinless and skinless chicken fillet
- 1 tablespoon butter
- 2 cloves of garlic, minced
- 2 tablespoons chopped fresh basil
- 8 grams of dry fettuccine
- salt and pepper to taste
- 2 tablespoons vegetable oil

Instructions
1. Once the butter is melted in a large pan over low heat, season with garlic and allow to simmer for 30 seconds. Add tomatoes and 3/4 cup chicken broth; and keep heating on a medium heat. Once the liquid starts to boil, reduce the heat and simmer for about 10 minutes without a lid or until the tomatoes are soft.
2. Add the cream and keep simmering until the sauce thickens.
3. Season with salt and pepper, the chicken on both sides. Heat oil in a large frying pan over medium-high heat and fry the chicken. Press the chicken occasionally with a slotted spatula. Bake for about 4 minutes per side. Set aside; cover and keep warm. Discard the fat from the pan.
4. In the same pan, bring to a boil 1/4 cup chicken broth over medium heat. Reduce slightly and add to the cream sauce; stir in the basil and adjust the seasonings to taste.

5. Meanwhile, boil a large pan with lightly salted water. Add fettuccine and cook for about 8 to 10 minutes or until al dente; drain, transfer to a bowl and mix with 3 to 4 tablespoons of sauce.
6. Cut each chicken fillet into 2 or 3 diagonal slices. Heat the sauce carefully if necessary. Transfer the pasta to serving trays; garnish with chicken and sprinkle with cream sauce to serve.

Macros
Per serving: 641 calories; 34.8 g total fat; 156 mg of cholesterol; 501 mg of sodium. 47 grams of carbohydrates 36.3 g of protein;

104. One Pan Orecchiette Pasta

Prep time: 15 minutes
Servings: 2
Ingredients
- 2 tablespoons olive oil
- 1/2 onion, diced
- salt to taste
- 8 grams of spicy Italian sausages
- 3 1/2 cups of low-sodium chicken broth, divided or as required
- 1 1/4 cup orecchiette pasta
- 1/2 cup chopped arugula
- 1/4 cup finely grated Parmigiano-Reggiano cheese

Instructions
1. Heat the olive oil in a deep frying pan over medium heat. Cook and stir the onion with a pinch of salt until soft and golden brown, 5 to 7 minutes. Stir the sausages with onions, 5 to 7 minutes.
2. Pour 1 1/2 cup chicken stock into the sausage mixture and bring to a boil. Add the pasta to the orecchiette; boil and mix the pasta in a warm broth, add the remaining broth when the liquid is absorbed until the pasta is well cooked, and most of the broth is absorbed, about 15 minutes.
3. Stir in the sausage mixture. Spread the pasta in bowls and sprinkle with Parmigiano-Reggiano cheese.

Macros
Per serving: 662 calories; 39.1 grams of fat; 46.2 g carbohydrates; 31.2 g of protein; 60 mg cholesterol; 1360 mg of sodium.

105. Rustic Pasta

Prep time: 25 minutes
Servings: 6

Ingredients

- 1 pound of rotini or pasta fusilli
- 6 slices of bacon
- 1/2 cup of extra virgin olive oil
- 2 medium onions, minced
- 1 red pepper, minced
- 1/4 cup chopped parsley
- 4 cloves of garlic, minced
- Salt (optional)
- 1/2 teaspoon of crushed red pepper flakes
- 1 can (28 ounces) of yellow tomatoes, unsalted, coarsely chopped
- 1/2 cup black or green ripe seedless olives, sliced and drained
- 2 tablespoons drained capers
- 1/2 teaspoon dried oregano
- 1/2 cup grated Parmesan cheese

Instructions

1. Cook the pasta according to the instructions on the package. Meanwhile, fry bacon in a deep frying pan until crispy. Drain the bacon on a paper towel; break into 1/2 inch pieces.
2. Discard the bacon juice from the pan; add the oil. Sauté onions in oil over medium heat for 5 minutes, stirring occasionally.
3. Add pepper, parsley, garlic, and pepper flakes; cook for 2 minutes. Add tomatoes and reserved bacon; simmer 10 minutes, stirring occasionally. Stir olives and oregano; simmer for 2 minutes. Season with salt, if desired.
4. Drain the pasta; mix with the sauce and cheese.

Macros

Per serving: 593 calories 27.6 g fat; 68.6 g carbohydrates; 17.8 g of protein; 16 mg of cholesterol; 770 mg of sodium.

106. Creamy Cajun Chicken Pasta

Prep time: 15 minutes
Servings: 2

Ingredients

- 4 oz linguine
- 2 boneless chicken fillets, skinless, cut into thin strips
- 2 teaspoons Cajun herbs
- 2 tablespoons butter
- 1 green pepper, minced
- ½ red pepper, minced
- 4 fresh chopped mushrooms
- 1 chopped green onion
- 1 ½ cups thick cream
- ¼ teaspoon dried basil
- ¼ teaspoon lemon pepper
- ¼ teaspoon salt
- 1 teaspoon garlic powder
- ⅛ teaspoon ground black pepper
- 2 tablespoons grated Parmesan cheese

Instructions

1. Boil lightly salted water in a large panAdd linguini and cook for 8 to 10 minutes or until al dente; drain.
2. In the meantime, put the chicken and Cajun herbs in a bowl and mix to coat.
3. Bake chicken in butter in a large frying pan over medium heat for 5 to 7 minutes. Add green and red peppers, chopped mushrooms, and green onions; cook 2 to 3 minutes. Reduce the heat and stir in the whipped cream. Season the sauce with basil, lemon pepper, salt, garlic powder, and ground black pepper and heat.
4. Mix the linguini with the sauce in a large bowl. Sprinkle with grated Parmesan cheese.

Macros

Per serving: 1109 calories 82.2 g total fat; 348 mg of cholesterol; 1134 mg of sodium. 53.7 g of carbohydrates; 42.7 g of protein.

CHAPTER 6: SEAFOOD & FISH RECIPES

Seafood and fish are rich in protein or for tissue construction. As this term is generally understood, it includes vertebrate fish such as salmon, cod, shad, etc., as well as other aquatic animals like lobsters, crabs, shrimp, oysters, and cockles. **Here are some recipes for seafood and fish:**

107. Grilled Marinated Shrimp

Prep time: 30 minutes

Servings: 6

Ingredients

- 1 cup olive oil
- 1/4 cup chopped fresh parsley
- 1 lemon, juiced
- 2 tablespoons hot pepper sauce
- 3 cloves of garlic, finely chopped
- 1 tablespoon tomato puree
- 2 teaspoons dried oregano
- 1 teaspoon salt
- 1 teaspoon ground black pepper
- 2 pounds of shrimp, peeled

Instructions

1. Combine olive oil, parsley, lemon juice, hot sauce, garlic, tomato puree, oregano, salt, and black pepper in a bowl. Reserve a small amount for later. Pour the rest of the marinade into a large, resealable plastic bag with shrimp. Close and marinate in the fridge for 2 hours.
2. Preheat the grill on medium heat. Thread shrimp on skewers, poke once at the tail, and once at the head. Discard the marinade.
3. Lightly oil the grill. Cook the shrimp for 5 minutes on each side or until they are opaque, often baste with the reserved marinade.

Macros

Per serving: 447 calories; 37.5 grams of fat; 3.7 grams of carbohydrates; 25.3 g of protein; 230 mg of cholesterol; 800 mg of sodium

108. Grilled Salmon

Prep time: 15 minutes

Servings: 6

Ingredients

- 1 1/2 pounds salmon fillet
- pepper to taste
- garlic powder to taste
- 1/3 cup soy sauce
- 1/3 cup of brown sugar
- 1/3 cup of water
- 1/4 cup vegetable oil

Instructions

1. Season the salmon fillets with lemon pepper, salt, and garlic powder.
2. Mix the soy sauce, brown sugar, water, and vegetable oil in a small bowl until the sugar is dissolved. Place the fish in a big resealable plastic bag with the soy sauce mixture, seal, and let marinate for at least 2 hours.
3. Preheat the grill on medium heat.
4. Lightly oil the grill then place the salmon and leave to cook for about 6 to 8 minutes each side or until the fish flakes easily with a fork.

Macros

Per serving: 318 calories; 20.1 grams of fat; 13.2 g carbohydrates; 20.5 g of protein; 56 mg cholesterol; 1092 mg of sodium

109. Cedar Planked Salmon

Prep time: 15 minutes

Servings: 6

Ingredients

- 3 untreated cedar boards
- 1/3 cup of vegetable oil
- 1/3 cup soy sauce
- 1/4 cup chopped green onions
- 1 1/2 tablespoon rice vinegar
- 1 teaspoon sesame oil
- 1 teaspoon finely chopped garlic
- 1 tablespoon grated fresh ginger root
- 2 skinless salmon fillets

Instructions

1. Soak the cedar boards in hot water for at least 1 hour. Enjoy longer if you have time.
2. Combine vegetable oil, rice vinegar, sesame oil, soy sauce, green onions, ginger, and garlic in a shallow dish. Place the salmon

fillits in the marinade and turn them over to coat them. Cover and marinate for a minimum of 15 minutes or a maximum of one hour.

3. Preheat an outside grill over medium heat. Place the shelves on the rack. The boards are ready when they start to smoke a little.
4. Place the salmon fillets on the shelves and discard the marinade — cover and grill for about 20 minutes. The fish is cooked if you can peel it with a fork.

Macros

Per serving: 678 calories; 45.8 g fat; 1.7 g carbohydrates; 61.3 g of protein; 179 mg cholesterol; 981 mg of sodium

110. **Broiled Tilapia Parmesan**

Prep time: 5 minutes

Servings: 8

Ingredients

- 1/2 cup Parmesan cheese
- 1/4 cup butter, soft
- 3 tablespoons mayonnaise
- 2 tablespoons fresh lemon juice
- 1/4 teaspoon dried basil
- 1/4 teaspoon ground black pepper
- 1/8 teaspoon onion powder
- 1/8 teaspoon celery salt
- 2 pounds Tilapia fillets

Instructions

1. Preheat the grill on your oven. Grease a drip tray or grill pan with aluminum foil.
2. Combine parmesan, butter, mayonnaise, and lemon juice in a small bowl. Season with dried basil, pepper, onion powder, and celery salt mixed well and set aside.
3. Place the fillets in a single layer on the prepared dish. Grill a few centimeters from the heat for 2 to 3 minutes, turn the fillets and grill for a few minutes. Remove the fillets from the oven and cover with the Parmesan cheese mixture on top. Grill for another 2 minutes or until the garnish is golden brown and fish flakes easily with a fork. Be careful not to overcook the fish.

Macros

Per serving: 224 calories; 12.8 g of fat; 0.8 g

carbohydrates; 25.4 g of protein; 63 mg cholesterol; 220 mg of sodium.

111. **Fish Tacos**

Prep time: 40 minutes

Servings: 8

Ingredients

- 1 cup flour
- 2 tablespoons corn flour
- 1 teaspoon baking powder
- 1/2 teaspoon of salt
- 1 egg
- 1 cup of beer
- 1/2 cup of yogurt
- 1/2 cup of mayonnaise
- 1 lime, juice
- 1 jalapeño pepper, minced
- 1 c. Finely chopped capers
- 1/2 teaspoon dried oregano
- 1/2 teaspoon ground cumin
- 1/2 teaspoon dried dill
- 1 teaspoon ground cayenne pepper
- 1 liter of oil for frying
- 1 pound of cod fillets, 2-3 ounces each
- 8 corn tortillas
- 1/2 medium cabbage, finely shredded

Instructions

1. Prepare beer dough: combine flour, corn flour, baking powder and salt in a large bowl. Mix the egg and the beer and stir in the flour mixture quickly.
2. To make a white sauce: combine yogurt and mayonnaise in a medium bowl. Gradually add fresh lime juice until it is slightly fluid — season with jalapeño, capers, oregano, cumin, dill, and cayenne pepper.
3. Heat the oil in a frying pan.
4. Lightly sprinkle the fish with flour. Dip it in the beer batter and fry until crispy and golden brown. Drain on kitchen paper. Heat the tortillas. Place the fried fish in a tortilla and garnish with grated cabbage and white sauce.

Macros

Per serving: 409 calories; 18.8 g of fat; 43 grams of carbohydrates 17.3 g of protein; 54 mg cholesterol; 407 mg of sodium.

112. Grilled Tilapia with Mango Salsa

Prep time: 45 minutes

Servings: 2

Ingredients

- 1/3 cup extra virgin olive oil
- 1 tablespoon lemon juice
- 1 tablespoon chopped fresh parsley
- 1 clove of garlic, minced
- 1 teaspoon dried basil
- 1 teaspoon ground black pepper
- 1/2 teaspoon salt
- 2 tilapia fillets (1 oz each)
- 1 large ripe mango, peeled, pitted and diced
- 1/2 red pepper, diced
- 2 tablespoons chopped red onion
- 1 tablespoon chopped fresh coriander
- 1 jalapeño pepper, seeded and minced
- 2 tablespoons lime juice
- 1 tablespoon lemon juice
- salt and pepper to taste

Instruction

1. Mix extra virgin olive oil, 1 tablespoon lemon juice, parsley, garlic, basil, 1 teaspoon pepper, and 1/2 teaspoon salt in a bowl, then pour into a resealable plastic bag. Add the tilapia fillets, cover with the marinade, remove excess air, and close the bag. Marinate in the fridge for 1 hour.
2. Prepare the mango salsa by combining the mango, red pepper, red onion, coriander, and jalapeño pepper in a bowl. Add the lime juice and 1 tablespoon lemon juice and mix well. Season with salt and pepper and keep until serving.
3. Preheat a grill over medium heat and lightly oil.
4. Remove the tilapia from the marinade and remove the excess. Discard the rest of the marinade. Grill the fillets until the fish is no longer translucent in the middle and flake easily with the fork for 3 to 4 minutes on each side, depending on the thickness of the fillets. Serve the tilapia topped with mango salsa.

Macros

Per serving: 634 calories; 40.2 grams of fat; 33.4 g carbohydrates; 36.3 g of protein; 62 mg cholesterol; 697 mg of sodium.

113. Seafood Linguine

Prep time: 45 minutes

Servings: 8

Ingredients

- 1 packet of linguine pasta
- ½ cup chopped red onion
- 3 teaspoons garlic powder
- 1/4 cup olive oil
- 3 cups milk
- 2 teaspoons chopped fresh parsley
- 1/2 cup chopped green pepper
- 1/2 cup chopped red pepper
- 1/2 cup broccoli florets
- 1/2 cup sliced carrots
- 1 cup chopped fresh mushrooms
- 1 cup canned shrimp
- 1 cup crabmeat, drained
- 1 pound scallops

Instructions

1. Boil lightly salted water in a large panAdd linguini and cook for 6 to 8 minutes, or until al dente. Drain.
2. Meanwhile, fry the red onion and garlic in olive oil in an electric frying pan or large frying pan. Add the milk when the onion is transparent. Boil until bubbles form on the edges of the pan. Add parsley, green and chopped red pepper, broccoli, carrots, mushrooms, shrimps, crab, and scallops and stir until well absorbed.
3. Remove 1/2 cup of milk from the mixture and place it in a small bowl with the flour. Stir until smooth. Return to the pan with seafood and vegetables. Let the mixture thicken. Season with salt and pepper.
4. Pour the fish sauce over the cooked and drained linguini noodles. Serve hot.

Macros

Per serving: 418 calories; 11 g of fat; 52 grams of carbohydrates, 28.2 g of protein; 69 mg of cholesterol; 242 mg of sodium.

114. Blackened Salmon Fillets

Prep time: 15 minutes

Servings: 4

Ingredients

- 2 tablespoons paprika powder
- 1 tablespoon cayenne pepper powder
- 1 tablespoon onion powder
- 2 teaspoons salt
- 1/2 teaspoon ground white pepper
- 1/2 teaspoon ground black pepper
- 1/4 teaspoon dried thyme
- 1/4 teaspoon dried basil
- 1/4 teaspoon dried oregano
- 4 salmon fillets, skin and bones removed
- 1/2 cup unsalted butter, melted

Instructions

1. Mix into a small bowl bell pepper, cayenne pepper, onion powder, salt, white pepper, black pepper, thyme, basil and oregano.
2. Spread 1/4 cup of butter on salmon fillets and season evenly with the cayenne pepper mixture.
3. Drizzle ½ of the remaining butter on each fillet.
4. Cook the salmon in a large heavy-bottomed pan on both sides until dark, 2 to 5 minutes and drizzle with remaining butter until the fish easily flakes with a fork.

Macros

Per serving: 511 calories; 38.3 grams of fat; 4.5 grams of carbohydrates 37.4 g of protein; 166 mg cholesterol; 1248 mg of sodium

115. Seafood Enchiladas

Prep time: 15 minutes

Servings: 6

Ingredients

- 1 onion, minced
- 1 tablespoon butter
- 1/2 pound of fresh crab meat
- 1/4 pound shrimp - peeled, gutted and coarsely chopped
- 8 grams of Colby cheese
- 6 flour tortillas (10 inches)
- 1 cup half and half cream
- 1/2 cup sour cream
- 1/4 cup melted butter
- 1 1/2 teaspoon dried parsley
- 1/2 teaspoon garlic salt

Instructions

1. Bring the oven up to 175 ° C (350 ° F).
2. Fry the onions in a large frying pan in 1 tablespoon butter until they are transparent. Remove the pan from the heat and stir in the crab meat and shrimp. Grate the cheese and mix half of the seafood.
3. Place a large spoon of the mixture in each tortilla. Roll the tortillas around the mixture and place them in a 9 x 13-inch baking dish.
4. In a saucepan over medium heat, combine half and half, sour cream, 1/4 cup butter, parsley and garlic salt. Stir until the mixture is lukewarm and mixed. Pour the sauce over the enchiladas and sprinkle with the remaining cheese.
5. Bake in the preheated oven for 30 minutes.

Macros

Per serving: 607 calories, 36.5 grams of fat; 42.6 g carbohydrates; 26.8 g of protein; 136 mg of cholesterol; 1078 mg of sodium.

116. Cajun Seafood Pasta

Prep time: 15 minutes

Servings: 6

Ingredients

- 2 cups of whipped cream
- 1 tsp chopped basil
- 1 tsp chopped fresh thyme
- 2 tsps salt
- 2 tsps ground black pepper
- 1 1/2 tsp red pepper flakes
- 1 tsp white pepper
- 1 cup minced green onions
- 1 cup minced parsley
- 1/2 peeled shrimp
- 1/2 cup scallops
- 1/2 cup of grated Swiss cheese
- 1/2 cup grated Parmesan cheese
- 1 pound dry fettuccine pasta

Instructions

1. Put the fettuccine in a big pot with boiling salted water until al dente.

2. In the meantime, pour the cream into a large skillet and cook over medium heat, constantly stirring until it boils.
3. Moderate heat and adjoin spices, salt, pepper, onions, and parsley. Allow to stew for 7 to 8 minutes or until thick.
4. Add the seafood and stir until shrimps are opaque.
5. Add the cheese and stir well.
6. Drain the pasta. Serve the sauce over the noodles.

Macros

Per serving: 695 calories; 36.7 grams of fat; 62.2 g carbohydrates; 31.5 g of protein; 193 mg cholesterol; 1054 mg of sodium

117. Seafood Stuffing

Prep time: 25 minutes
Servings: 8
Ingredients

- 1/2 cup butter
- 1/2 cup chopped green pepper
- 1/2 cup chopped onion
- 1/2 cup chopped celery
- Drained and flaky crabmeat
- 1/2 pound of medium-sized shrimp - peeled and deveined
- 1/2 cup spiced and seasoned breadcrumbs
- 1 mixture of filling for cornbread
- 2 tablespoons of white sugar, divided
- 1 can of mushroom soup (10.75 ounces) condensed
- 14.5 oz chicken broth

Instructions

1. Melt the butter in a large frying pan over medium heat. Add pepper, onion, celery crabmeat and shrimp; boil and stir for about 5 minutes. Set aside.
2. In a large bowl, mix stuffing, breadcrumbs, and 1 tablespoon sugar. Stir the vegetables and seafood from the pan. Add the mushroom cream and as much chicken broth as you want. Pour into a 9 x 13-inch baking dish.
3. Bake in the preheated oven for 30 minutes or until lightly roasted.

Macros

Per serving: 344 calories; 15.7 grams of fat; 28.4 g of carbohydrates; 22 g of protein; 94 mg of cholesterol; 1141 mg of sodium.

118. Scrumptious Salmon Cakes

Prep time: 15 minutes
Servings: 8
Ingredients

- 2 cans of salmon, drained and crumbled
- 3/4 cup Italian breadcrumbs
- 1/2 cup chopped fresh parsley
- 2 eggs, beaten
- 2 green onions, minced
- 2 teaspoons seafood herbs
- 1 1/2 teaspoon ground black pepper
- 1 1/2 teaspoons garlic powder
- 3 tablespoons Worcestershire sauce
- 2 tablespoons Dijon mustard
- 3 tablespoons grated Parmesan
- 2 tablespoons creamy vinaigrette
- 1 tablespoon olive oil

Instructions

1. Combine salmon, breadcrumbs, parsley, eggs, green onions, seafood herbs, black pepper, garlic powder, Worcestershire sauce, parmesan cheese, Dijon mustard, and creamy vinaigrette; divide and shape into eight patties.
2. Heat olive oil in a large frying pan over medium heat. Bake the salmon patties in portions until golden brown, 5 to 7 minutes per side. Repeat if necessary with more olive oil.

Macros

Per serving: 263 calories; 12.3 g fat; 10.8 g of carbohydrates; 27.8 g of protein; 95 mg cholesterol; 782 mg of sodium

119. Easy Tuna Patties

Prep time: 15 minutes
Servings: 4
Ingredients

- 2 teaspoons lemon juice
- 3 tablespoons grated Parmesan
- 2 eggs
- 10 tablespoons Italian breadcrumbs
- 3 tuna cans, drained
- 3 tablespoons diced onion
- 1 pinch of ground black pepper
- 3 tablespoons vegetable oil

Instructions

1. Beat the eggs and lemon juice in a bowl. Stir in the Parmesan cheese and breadcrumbs to obtain a paste. Add tuna and onion until everything is well mixed. Season with black pepper. Form the tuna mixture into eight 1-inch-thick patties.
2. Heat the vegetable oil in a frying pan over medium heat; fry the patties until golden brown, about 5 minutes on each side.

Macros

Per serving: 325 calories; 15.5 grams of fat; 13.9 g of carbohydrates; 31.3 g of protein; 125 mg cholesterol; 409 mg of sodium.

120. Heather's Grilled Salmon

Prep time: 10 minutes
Servings: 4
Ingredients

- 1/4 cup brown sugar
- 1/4 cup olive oil
- 1/4 cup soy sauce
- 2 teaspoons lemon pepper
- 1 teaspoon dried thyme
- 1 teaspoon dried basil
- 1 teaspoon dried parsley
- 1/2 teaspoon garlic powder
- 4 (6 oz) salmon fillets

Instruction

1. In a cup, whisk the brown sugar, olive oil, soy sauce, lemon pepper, thyme, basil, parsley, and garlic powder together and dump into a plastic resealable container.
2. Add salmon fillets, marinade cover, pinch excess air and close the container. Marinate for at least 1 hour in the refrigerator, turning over periodically.
3. For medium heat, preheat an outdoor barbecue, and gently spray the grate. Pick the salmon and shake off fat from the marinade. Discard the marinade left over.
4. Grill the salmon until browned on the preheated grill and the fish flakes quickly with a fork, about 5 minutes on each side.

Macros

Per serving: 380 calories; 19.4 g fat; 15.7 g carbohydrates; 34.7 g protein; 88 mg cholesterol; 1251 mg sodium.

121. Brown Butter Perch

Prep time: 15 minutes
Servings: 4
Ingredients

- 1 cup flour
- 1 teaspoon salt
- 1/2 teaspoon finely ground black pepper
- 1/2 teaspoon cayenne pepper
- 8 oz fresh perch fillets
- 2 tablespoons butter
- 1 lemon cut in half

Instructions

1. In a bowl, beat flour, salt, black pepper, and cayenne pepper. Gently squeeze the perch fillets into the flour mixture to coat well and remove excess flour.
2. Heat the butter in a frying pan over medium heat until it is foamy and brown hazel. Place the fillets in portions in the pan and cook them light brown, about 2 minutes on each side. Place the cooked fillets on a plate, squeeze the lemon juice, and serve.

Macros

Per serving: 271 calories; 11.5 g of fat; 30.9 g of carbohydrates; 12.6 g of protein; 43 mg of cholesterol; 703 mg of sodium.

122. Red Snapper Veracruz

Prep time: 15 minutes
Servings: 2
Ingredients

- 2 tablespoons olive oil
- 1/2 white onion, diced
- 3 cloves of garlic, minced
- 1 tablespoon capers
- 1 tablespoon caper juice
- 1 cup cherry tomatoes, cut in half
- 1/3 cup pitted and sliced green olives
- 1 jalapeño pepper, seeded and minced
- 2 teaspoons fresh chopped oregano
- 2 teaspoons of olive oil
- 2 red snapper fillets, sliced in half
- salt and pepper to taste
- 1/2 teaspoon cayenne pepper,
- 2 limes, juiced

Instructions

1. Preheat the oven to 220 ° C.
2. Heat the olive oil in a frying pan over medium heat. Stir in the onion; cook and <u>stir</u>

until onions begin to become transparent, 6 to 7 minutes.

3. Cook and stir garlic until fragrant (30 seconds). Add the capers and the caper juice; stir to combine.

4. Stir in the tomatoes, olives, and jalapeño. Boil and stir for about 3 minutes. Remove from the heat; mix in the oregano.

5. Pour 1 tsp of olive oil into a small baking dish. Sprinkle 1 tbsp of the tomato-olive mixture. Moisten with salt, black pepper, and cayenne pepper. Add with more filling and juice of 1 lime. Repeat with the rest of the snapper fillet, herbs, and lime juice in a second baking dish.

6. Bake in the preheated kiln until the fish is flaky and no longer translucent, 15 to 20 minutes.

Macros

Per serving: 452 calories; 25.2 g fat; 16.2 g carbohydrates; 43.1 g of protein; 73 mg of cholesterol; 1034 mg of sodium.

123. Baked Seafood Au Gratin

Prep time: 20 minutes
Servings: 8
Ingredients

- 1 onion, chopped
- 1 green pepper, chopped
- 1 cup butter, divided
- 1 cup flour, divided
- 1 pound of fresh crab meat
- 4 cups of water
- 1 pound of fresh shrimp, peeled
- 1/2 pound scallops
- 1/2 pound plaice fillets
- 3 cups of milk
- 1 cup grated cheddar cheese
- 1 tablespoon distilled white vinegar
- 1 teaspoon Worcestershire sauce
- 1/2 teaspoon of salt
- 1 pinch of ground black pepper
- 1 pinch of hot pepper sauce
- 1/2 cup of grated Parmesan cheese

Instruction

1. In a heavy skillet, fry onion, and pepper in 1/2 cup butter. Cook until soft. Mix in 1/2 cup flour and cook over medium heat for 10 minutes, stirring regularly. Stir in crab meat, remove from heat and set aside.

2. Boil the water in a large pot. Add shrimp, scallops, and plaice and simmer for 3 minutes. Drain, reserving 1 cup of cooking liquid.

3. Melt the remaining butter in a saucepan half over low heat. Stir in 1/2 cup remaining flour. Cook, stirring constantly for 1 minute. Gradually add the milk and the reserved liquid. Increase the heat to medium; boil, constantly stirring until the mixture thickens and bubbles. Add grated cheddar cheese, vinegar, Worcestershire sauce, salt, pepper, and hot sauce. Stir in cooked seafood.

4. Bring the oven up to 175 ° C (350 ° F). Butter a 9 x 13-inch light baking dish. Squeeze the crabmeat mixture into the bottom of the prepared pan. Place the seafood mixture over the crabmeat crust and sprinkle with Parmesan cheese.

5. Bake in the preheated oven for 30 minutes or until light brown. Serve immediately.

Macros

Per serving: 566 calories; 34.2 g fat; 20.4 g carbohydrates; 42.8 g of protein; 233 mg cholesterol; 859 mg of sodium.

124. Fish & Chips

Prep time: 5 minutes
Servings: 4
Ingredients

- 1 liter of vegetable oil for frying
- Red snapper fillets (1 pound)
- 1 beaten egg
- 1/2 cup dry breadcrumbs

Instruction

- Heat the oil in a large frying pan.
- Dip the fillets in the beaten egg and place in breadcrumbs.
- Slowly slide the fish into the hot oil and fry until golden brown. Drain on kitchen paper. Serve hot.

Macros

Per serving: 386 calories; 26.2 g fat; 9.8 g of carbohydrates; 26.8 g of protein; 92 mg of cholesterol; 175 mg of sodium

125. Fish Taquitos

Prep time: 30 minutes
Servings: 6
Ingredients

- Fish fillets (one pound)
- 12 corn tortillas (6 inch)
- 1/4 cup canola oil
- 1/4 cup lemon juice
- 1 clove of garlic minced
- 1 teaspoon dried oregano
- 1 teaspoon Cajun herbs
- 1 cup grated cheddar cheese
- 2 liters of vegetable oil for frying

Instructions

1. Cut the fish into strips that are 3/4 inch thick and 3 inches long. Mix canola oil, lemon juice, garlic, oregano, and Cajun spice mixture in a plastic container. Place the fish strips in a container and marinate for 1 hour.
2. Heat the tortillas in the microwave.
3. Drain the marinade. Place a strip of fish on one end of a tortilla, roll well and fix with a toothpick.
4. Heat the oil in a frying pan. The taquitos dive into the hot oil. Bake until golden brown, no more than 3 or 4 minutes each. Drain on kitchen paper.
5. Place the taquitos in a baking dish. Sprinkle with grated cheese.
6. Bake at 350 degrees F (175 degrees C) for 5 minutes or until cheese is melted.

Macros

Per serving: 642 calories; 51.3 g of fat; 25.1 g carbohydrates; 22.4 g of protein; 55 mg cholesterol; 295 mg of sodium

126. Fish in Foil

Prep time: 10 m
Servings: 2 servings
Ingredients

- 2 fillets of rainbow trout
- 1 tablespoon of olive oil
- 2 teaspoons of salt with garlic
- 1 teaspoon ground black pepper
- 1 fresh jalapeño pepper, sliced
- 1 lemon cut into slices

Instructions

1. Heat up the oven to 200 degrees C (400 degrees F). Rinse and dry the fish.
2. Rub the fillets with olive oil and season with garlic salt and black pepper. Lay each on a large sheet of aluminum foil. Garnish with jalapeño slices and squeeze the juice from the lemon onto the fish. Place the lemon slices on the fillets. Carefully seal all edges of the foil to form closed bags. Place the packages on a baking sheet.
3. Bake in the preheated oven for 15 to 20 minutes, depending on the size of the fish. The fish is cooked when it easily breaks with a fork.

Macros

Per serving: 213 calories; 10.9 g fat; 7.5 grams of carbohydrates; 24.3 g of protein; 67 mg of cholesterol; 1850 mg of sodium.

CHAPTER 7: EGG RECIPES

Eggs are a widely used ingredient in many households. It is, therefore, useful to have many tasty egg recipes in your kitchen arsenal. This encourages variation in your meals and can promote a balanced diet for the family. Eggs are, in most cases, a food that is universally appreciated by adults and children.

Let's look at some egg recipes:

127. Denver Fried Omelet

Prep time: 10 minutes

Servings: 4

Ingredients

- 2 tablespoons butter
- 1/2 onion, minced
- 1/2 green pepper, minced
- 1 cup chopped cooked ham
- 8 eggs
- 1/4 cup of milk
- 1/2 cup grated cheddar cheese
- ground black pepper to taste

Instructions

1. Preheat the oven to 200 degrees C (400 degrees F). Grease a 10-inch round baking dish.
2. Melt the butter in a large frying pan over medium heat; cook and stir onion and pepper until soft, about 5 minutes. Stir in the ham and keep cooking for 5 minutes.
3. Beat the eggs and milk in a large bowl. Stir in the cheddar cheese and ham; Season with salt and black pepper. Pour the mixture into a prepared baking dish.
4. Bake in the preheated oven for about 25 minutes. Serve hot.

Macros

Per serving: 345 calories; 26.8 g of fat; 3.6 g carbohydrates; 22.4 g of protein; 381 mg of cholesterol; 712 mg of sodium.

128. Sausage Pan

Prep time: 25 minutes

Servings: 12

Ingredients

- 1 pound Breakfast Sausage
- 3 cups grated potatoes, drained and squeezed
- 1/4 cup melted butter
- 12 oz soft grated Cheddar cheese

- 1/2 cup onion, grated
- 1 (16 oz) small cottage cheese container
- 6 large eggs

Instructions

1. Preheat the oven to 190 ° C. Grease a 9 x 13-inch square oven dish lightly.
2. Fry the sausage in a deep frying pan over medium heat. Drain, crumble, and set aside.
3. Mix the grated potatoes and butter in the prepared baking dish. Cover the bottom and sides of the dish with the mixture. Combine sausage, cheddar, onion, cottage cheese, and eggs in a bowl. Pour over the potato mixture.
4. Bake in the preheated oven for 1 hour or until a toothpick in the center of the pan comes out clean. Allow cooling for 5 minutes before serving.

Macros

Per serving: 355 calories; 26.3 g of fat; 7.9 g of carbohydrates; 21.6 g of protein; 188 mg cholesterol; 755 mg of sodium.

129. Sausage Egg Casserole

Prep time: 20 minutes

Servings: 12 Servings

Ingredients

- 3/4-pound finely chopped pork sausage, 1 tablespoon butter, 4 green onions, minced
- 1/2 pound of fresh mushrooms, 10 eggs, beaten, 1 container (16 grams) low-fat cottage cheese
- 1 pound of Monterey Jack Cheese, grated, 2 cans of a green pepper diced, drained
- 1 cup flour, 1 teaspoon baking powder
- 1/2 teaspoon salt, 1/3 cup melted butter

Instructions

1. Place the sausage in a large deep frying pan. Bake over medium heat until smooth. Drain and set aside. Melt the butter in a pan, cook

and stir the green onions and mushrooms until they are soft.

2. Combine eggs, cottage cheese, Monterey Jack cheese, and peppers in a large bowl. Stir in sausages, green onions, and mushrooms. Cover and refrigerate overnight.

3. Bring the oven up to 175 ° C (350 ° F). Grease a 9 x 13-inch light baking dish.

4. Sift the flour, baking powder, and salt into a bowl. Stir in the melted butter. Stir the flour mixture into the egg mixture. Pour into the prepared baking dish.

5. Bake in the preheated oven for 40 to 50 minutes or until lightly browned. Let stand for 10 minutes before serving.

Macros

Per serving: 408 calories; 28.7 grams of fat; 12.4 g carbohydrates; 25.2 g of protein; 224 mg of cholesterol; 1095 mg of sodium.

130. **Baked Omelet Squares**

Prep time: 15 minutes
Servings: 8

Ingredients

- 1/4 cup butter
- 1 small onion, minced
- 1 1/2 cups grated cheddar cheese
- 1 can of sliced mushrooms
- 1 can sliced black olives
- cooked ham (optional)
- sliced jalapeño peppers (optional)
- 12 eggs, scrambled
- 1/2 cup of milk
- salt and pepper to taste

Instructions

1. Preheat the oven to 205 ° C (400 ° F). Grease a 9 x 13-inch baking dish.

2. Melt the butter in a frying pan over medium heat and cook the onion until done.

3. Spread cheddar cheese on the bottom of the prepared baking dish. Layer with mushrooms, olives, fried onion, ham, and jalapeño peppers. Stir the eggs in a bowl with milk, salt, and pepper. Pour the egg mixture over the ingredients, but do not mix.

4. Bake in the preheated oven, uncovered, for 30 minutes. Let it cool slightly, then cut it into squares and serve.

Macros

Per serving: 344 calories; 27.3 g fat; 7.2 grams of carbohydrates; 17.9 g of protein; 254 mg of cholesterol; 1087 mg of sodium.

131. **Ken's Hard-Boiled Eggs**

Prep time: 5 minutes
Servings: 8

Ingredients

- 1 tablespoon of salt
- 1/4 cup distilled white vinegar
- 6 cups of water
- 8 eggs

Instructions

1. Mix the salt, vinegar, and water in a large saucepan and bring to a boil over high heat. Add the eggs one by one, and be careful not to split them. Lower the heat and cook over low heat and cook for 14 minutes.

2. Remove the eggs from the hot water and place them in a container filled with ice water or cold water. Cool completely, approximately 15 minutes. Store in the refrigerator for up to 1 week.

Macros

Per serving: 72 calories; 5 grams of fat; 0.4 g carbohydrates 6.3 g protein; 186 mg of cholesterol; 947 mg of sodium.

132. **Pepperoni Eggs**

Prep time: 10 minutes
Servings: 2 Servings

Ingredients

- 1 cup of egg substitute
- 1 egg
- 3 green onions, minced
- 8 slices of pepperoni, diced
- 1/2 teaspoon of garlic powder
- 1 teaspoon melted butter
- 1/4 cup grated Romano cheese
- 1 pinch of salt and ground black pepper to taste

Instruction

1. Combine the egg substitute, egg, green onions, pepperoni slices, and garlic powder in a bowl.

2. Heat the butter in a non-stick frying pan over low heat. Add the egg mixture, cover the pan and cook until the eggs are set, 10 to 15 minutes. Sprinkle Romano cheese on eggs and season with salt and pepper.

Macros

Per serving: 266 calories; 16.2 g fat; 3.7 grams of carbohydrates; 25.3 g of protein; 124 mg of cholesterol; 586 mg of sodium

133. Egg Cupcakes

Prep time: 15 minutes
Servings: 6
Ingredients

- 1 pack of bacon (12 ounces)
- 6 eggs
- 2 tablespoons of milk
- 1 c. Melted butter
- 1/4 teaspoon dried parsley
- 1/4 teaspoon salt
- 1/4 teaspoon ground black pepper
- 1/2 cup diced ham
- 1/4 cup grated mozzarella cheese
- 6 slices gouda

Instructions

1. Bring the oven up to 175 ° C (350 ° F).
2. Place the bacon in a large frying pan and cook over medium heat, occasionally turning until brown, about 5 minutes. Drain the bacon slices on kitchen paper.
3. Cover 6 cups of the non-stick muffin pan with slices of bacon.
4. Cut the remaining bacon slices and sprinkle the bottom of each cup.
5. In a large bowl, beat eggs, milk, butter, parsley, salt, and pepper. Stir in the ham and mozzarella cheese.
6. Pour the egg mixture into cups filled with bacon; garnish with Gouda cheese.
7. Bake in the preheated oven until Gouda cheese is melted and the eggs are tender for about 15 minutes.

Macros

Per serving: 310 calories; 22.9 g of fat; 2.1 g carbohydrates; 23.1 g of protein; 249 mg of cholesterol; 988 mg of sodium.

134. Dinosaur Eggs

Prep time: 20 minutes
Servings: 4
Ingredients
Mustard sauce:

- 1/4 cup coarse mustard
- 1/4 cup Greek yogurt
- 1 teaspoon garlic powder
- 1 pinch of cayenne pepper

Eggs:

- 2 beaten eggs
- 2 cups of mashed potato flakes
- 4 boiled eggs, peeled
- 1 can (15 oz) minced beef
- 2 liters of vegetable oil for frying

Instructions

1. Combine the old-fashioned mustard, Greek yogurt, garlic powder, and cayenne pepper in a small bowl until smooth.
2. Place 2 beaten eggs in a shallow dish; place the potato flakes in a separate shallow dish.
3. Divide the minced meat into 4 servings. Form salted beef around each egg until it is completely wrapped.
4. Roll the wrapped eggs in the beaten egg and brush with mashed potatoes until they are covered.
5. Heat the oil in a frying pan or large saucepan at 190 ° C (375 ° F).
6. Put 2 eggs in the hot oil and bake for 3 to 5 minutes until brown. Remove with a spoon and place on a plate lined with kitchen paper. Repeat this with the remaining 2 eggs.
7. Cut lengthwise and serve with mustard sauce.

Macros

Per serving: 784 calories; 63.2 grams of fat; 34 grams of carbohydrates 19.9 g of protein; 333 mg of cholesterol; 702 mg of sodium.

135. Zucchini with Egg

Prep time: 5 minutes
Servings: 2
Ingredients

- 1 1/2 tablespoons olive oil
- 2 large zucchini, cut into large chunks
- salt and ground black pepper to taste
- 2 large eggs
- 1 teaspoon water

Instruction

1. Heat the oil in a frying pan over medium heat; sauté zucchini until soft, about 10 minutes. Season the zucchini with salt and black pepper.
2. Beat the eggs with a fork in a bowl. Add water and beat until everything is well mixed. Pour the eggs over the zucchini; boil and stir for about 5 minutes.
3. Season zucchini and eggs with salt and black pepper.

Macros

Per serving: 213 calories; 15.7 grams of fat; 11.2 g carbohydrates; 10.2 g of protein; 186 mg of cholesterol; 180 mg of sodium.

136. Cheesy Amish Breakfast Casserole

Prep time: 10 minutes
Servings: 12
Ingredients

- 1 pound sliced bacon, diced
- 1 sweet onion, minced
- 4 cups grated and frozen potatoes, thawed
- 9 lightly beaten eggs
- 2 cups of grated cheddar cheese
- 1 1/2 cup of cottage cheese
- 1 1/4 cups of grated Swiss cheese

Instructions

1. Bring the oven up to 175 ° C (350 ° F). Grease a 9 x 13-inch baking dish.
2. Heat up a large frying pan over medium heat; cook the bacon and onion until the bacon is evenly browned, about 10 minutes. Drain.
3. Place the bacon and onion in a large bowl. Stir in potatoes, eggs, cheddar cheese, cottage cheese, and Swiss cheese. Pour the mixture into a prepared baking dish.
4. Bake in the preheated oven until the eggs are cooked and the cheese is melted 45 to 50 minutes. Let stand for 10 minutes before cutting and serving.

Macros

Per serving: 314 calories; 22.8 g of fat; 12.1 g carbohydrates; 21.7 g of protein; 188 mg cholesterol; 609 mg of sodium.

137. Benababs Eggs

Prep time: 1 hour
Servings: 4
Ingredients

- 1 tablespoon olive oil
- 2 tablespoons white vinegar
- 1 pint of water
- 4 artichokes, uncooked and cut into the heart
- 1 Hollandaise sauce recipe
- 4 eggs
- 1 cup black olives, sliced
- 1/2 cup chopped fresh chives

Instructions

1. Bring olive oil, 1 tablespoon of vinegar and water to a boil in a large pot. Put the artichoke hearts in the mixture and cook for 30 minutes or until soft; drain.
2. Prepare the Hollandaise sauce according to the recipe instructions.
3. Fill a large pot with 3 centimeters of water. Let the water simmer and add the remaining vinegar. Carefully break the eggs in the simmering water and cook for 3 to 5 minutes. The yellow must still be soft in the middle. Remove the eggs from the water with a spoon to drain and place them on a hot plate.
4. Place the artichoke hearts on a scale. Place a poached egg on each artichoke heart. Cover with hollandaise sauce. Sprinkle the olives with the sauce. Sprinkle the chives around the tray.

Macros

Per serving: 204 calories; 12.4 g fat; 16.3 g carbohydrates; 11 g of protein; 186 mg of cholesterol; 508 mg of sodium

CHAPTER 8: VEGETARIAN RECIPES

Vegetarian recipes are tasty and easy to prepare. You can turn any recipe into a pure vegetarian formula by replacing meat with a vegetarian alternative. Vegetarian dishes are also easier to digest and consume, and those who regularly eat vegetarian options have fewer health problems than those who eat meat. Plants are the basis of the food chain, closest to the source of life itself, namely solar energy. Green vegetables contain essential vitamins and minerals and are therefore beneficial for health.

Many people have switched to a vegetarian diet as a healthy way to lose weight. A diet rich in fruit and vegetables is indeed a smart strategy for weight loss.

By following a few simple vegetarian recipes, you can improve your health without much effort!

138. Mushrooms with Soy Sauce Glaze

Prep time: 5 minutes

Servings: 2

Ingredients

- 2 tablespoons butter
- 1 (8 oz) package sliced white mushrooms
- 2 cloves garlic, minced
- 2 teaspoons soy sauce
- ground black pepper to taste

Instructions

1. Melt the butter in a frying pan over medium heat; add the mushrooms; cook and stir until the mushrooms are soft and released about 5 minutes.
2. Stir in the garlic; keep cooking and stir for 1 minute. Pour the soy sauce; cook the mushrooms in the soy sauce until the liquid has evaporated, about 4 minutes.

Macros

Per serving: 135 calories; 11.9 g of fat; 5.4 g carbohydrates; 4.2 g of protein; 31 mg of cholesterol; 387 mg of sodium

139. California Grilled Vegetable Sandwich

Prep time: 30 minutes

Servings: 4

Ingredients

- 1/4 cup mayonnaise
- 3 garlic cloves, minced
- 1 tablespoon lemon juice
- 1/8 cup olive oil
- 1 cup sliced red peppers
- 1 small zucchini, sliced
- 1 red onion, sliced
- 1 small yellow pumpkin, sliced
- 2 pieces of focaccia bread (4 x 6 inch), split horizontally
- 1/2 cup of crumbled feta cheese

Instructions

1. Combine the mayonnaise, chopped garlic and lemon juice in a bowl. Chill in the fridge.
2. Preheat the grill on high heat.
3. Brush the vegetables with olive oil on each side. Brush the grill with oil. Place the pepper and zucchini closest to the center of the grill and add the onions and squash pieces. Bake for about 3 minutes, turn around and cook for another 3 minutes. Peppers can take a little longer. Remove from the grill and set aside.
4. Spread a little mayonnaise mixture on the sliced sides of the bread and sprinkle with feta cheese. Place the cheese on the grill and cover with the lid for 2 to 3 minutes.
5. Remove from the grill and brush with the vegetables. Enjoy open face grilled sandwiches.

Macros

Per serving: 393 calories; 23.8 g of fat; 36.5 g carbohydrates; 9.2 g of protein; 22 mg cholesterol; 623 mg of sodium

140. Fluffy Pancakes

Prep time: 10 minutes
Servings: 4
Ingredients

- 3/4 cup milk
- 2 tablespoons white vinegar
- 1 cup flour
- 2 tablespoons white sugar
- 1 teaspoon baking powder
- 1/2 teaspoon baking powder
- 1/2 teaspoon of salt
- 1 egg
- 2 tablespoons butter, melted
- cooking spray

Instructions

1. Mix the milk and vinegar in a medium bowl and let stand for 5 minutes.
2. Combine flour, sugar, baking powder, baking powder, and salt in a large bowl. Beat the egg and the butter in the sour milk. Pour the flour mixture into the moist ingredients and beat.
3. Heat up a large frying pan over medium heat and brush with cooking spray. Pour 1/4 cup of dough into the pan and cook until bubbles appear on the surface. Turn with a spatula and cook until gold on the other side.

Macros

Per serving: 230 calories; 8.2 g fat; 32.7 g carbohydrates; 6.4 g of protein; 65 mg of cholesterol; 650 mg of sodium

141. Delicious Sweet Potato Casserole

Prep time: 30 minutes
Servings: 12
Ingredients

- 4 cups sweet potatoes, diced
- 1/2 cup white sugar
- 2 beaten eggs
- 1/2 teaspoon of salt
- 4 tablespoons of soft butter
- 1/2 cup milk
- 1/2 teaspoon vanilla extract
- 1/2 cup packed brown sugar
- 1/3 cup all-purpose flour
- 3 tablespoons butter
- 1/2 cup soft chopped pecans

Instructions

1. Preheat the oven to 165 ° C (325 ° F). Put the sweet potatoes in a medium-sized pan with water to cover. Cook over medium heat until soft; drain and crush.
2. Combine sweet potatoes, white sugar, eggs, salt, butter, milk, and vanilla extract in a large bowl. Mix until smooth. Transfer to a 9 x 13-inch baking dish.
3. Combine brown sugar and flour in a medium bowl. Cut the butter until the mixture is coarse. Stir in the pecans. Now sprinkle the mixture over the sweet potato mixture.
4. Bake in the preheated oven for 30 minutes or until light brown.

Macros

Per serving: 226 calories; 11.1 grams of fat; 30.1 g carbohydrates; 2.9 g of protein; 50 mg cholesterol; 187 mg of sodium.

142. Light and Fluffy Spinach Quiche

Prep time: 20 minutes
Servings: 6
Ingredients

- 1/2 cup light mayonnaise
- 1/2 cup milk
- 4 lightly beaten eggs
- 8 oz grated cheddar cheese
- 1 packet of chopped spinach frozen, thawed and drained
- 1/4 cup chopped onion 1
- 1 (9-inch) uncooked pie crust

Instructions

1. Preheat the oven to 200 degrees C (400 degrees F). Cover a baking sheet with aluminum foil.
2. In a large bowl, mix mayonnaise and milk until smooth. Stir in the eggs. Arrange the spinach, cheese, and onion in the pie and form several layers. Pour in the egg mixture. Place the quiche on the prepared baking sheet. Cover the quiche with aluminum foil.
3. Bake for 45 minutes in the preheated oven. Remove the lid and bake for 10 to 15 minutes or until the top is golden brown.

Macros

Per serving: 356 calories; 23.2 g fat; 19.9 g of carbohydrates; 17.9 g of protein; 141 mg cholesterol; 612 mg of sodium.

143. Hot Artichoke and Spinach Dip

Prep time: 15 minutes
Servings: 12

Ingredients

- 1/4 cup mayonnaise
- 1 (8-oz) package cream cheese, softened
- 1/4 cup grated Parmesan cheese
- 1/4 cup grated Romano cheese
- 1 clove garlic, peeled and minced
- 1/2 teaspoon dried basil
- 1/4 teaspoon garlic
- salt and pepper to taste
- 1 (14-oz) can artichoke hearts, drained and chopped
- 1/2 cup frozen chopped spinach, thawed and drained
- 1/4 cup shredded mozzarella cheese

Instructions

1. Preheat oven to 350 degrees F (175 degrees C). Lightly grease a small baking dish.
2. In a medium bowl, mix together cream cheese, mayonnaise, Parmesan cheese, Romano cheese, garlic, basil, garlic salt, salt, and pepper. Gently stir in artichoke hearts and spinach.
3. Transfer the mixture to the prepared baking dish. Top with mozzarella cheese. Bake in the preheated oven for 25 minutes, until bubbly and lightly browned.

Macros

Per serving: 134 calories; 11.7 g fat; 3.4 g carbohydrates; 4.4 g protein; 28 mg cholesterol; 315 mg sodium.

144. Harvest Salad

Prep time: 15 minutes
Servings: 6

Ingredients

- 1/2 cup chopped nuts
- 1 bunch of spinach, rinsed and torn into bite-sized pieces
- 1/2 cup dried cranberries

- 1/2 cup of crumbled blue cheese
- 2 tomatoes, minced
- 1 avocado - peeled, seeded and diced
- 1/2 red onion, thinly sliced
- 2 tablespoons red raspberry jam (with seeds)
- 2 tablespoons red wine vinegar
- 1/3 cup walnut oil
- freshly ground black pepper
- salt

Instructions

1. Preheat the oven to 190 ° C. Place the nuts in a single layer on a baking sheet. Grill in the oven for 5 minutes or until the nuts start to turn brown.
2. Combine spinach, walnuts, cranberries, blue cheese, tomatoes, avocado, and red onion in a large bowl.
3. Mix jam, vinegar, walnut oil, pepper, and salt in a small bowl. Pour the salad dressing just before serving and mix well.

Macros

Per serving: 338 calories; 27.1 grams of fat; 22.1 grams of carbohydrates; 6.7 g of protein; 8 mg of cholesterol; 207 mg of sodium.

145. Spicy Bean Salsa

Prep time: 10 minutes
Servings: 12

Ingredients

- 1 (15 oz) can black eyed peas
- 1 (15 oz) can black beans, rinsed and drained
- 1 can of whole-grain corn, drained
- 1/2 cup chopped onion
- 1/2 cup chopped green pepper
- 1 can diced jalapeño pepper
- 1 can of tomato cubes, drained
- 1 cup of Italian dressing
- 1/2 teaspoon of garlic salt

Instruction

1. In a medium bowl, mix black eyed peas, black beans, corn, onion, green pepper, jalapeño peppers, and tomatoes. Season with Italian dressing and salt with garlic; mix well. Cover and put in the fridge overnight to mix the flavors.

Macros

Per serving: 155 calories; 6.4 g fat; 20.4 g carbohydrates; 5 g of protein; 0 mg cholesterol; 949

mg of sodium.

146. Sweet Potato Casserole Dessert

Prep time: 20 minutes
Servings: 18
Ingredients

- 4 1/2 cups of cooked and mashed sweet potatoes
- 1/2 cup melted butter
- 1/3 cup milk
- 1 cup white sugar
- 1/2 teaspoon vanilla extract
- 2 eggs, beaten
- 1 cup light brown sugar
- 1/2 cup all-purpose flour
- 1/3 cup butter
- 1 cup chopped pecans

Instructions

1. Bring the oven up to 175 ° C (350 ° F). Grease a 9 x 13-inch baking dish.
2. Combine mashed potatoes, 1/2 cup butter, milk, sugar, vanilla extract, and eggs in a large bowl. Spread the sweet potato mixture in the prepared baking dish.
3. Combine brown sugar and flour in a small bowl. Add 1/3 cup butter until the mixture is crumbly and add the pecans. Sprinkle the pecan mixture over the sweet potatoes.
4. Bake in the preheated oven for 25 minutes or until golden brown.

Macros

Per serving: 309 calories; 15.3 g fat; 41.9 g carbohydrates; 3.2 g of protein; 49 mg cholesterol; 103 mg of sodium

147. Spinach Quiche

Prep time: 20 minutes
Servings: 6
Ingredients

- 1/2 cup butter
- 3 cloves of garlic, minced
- 1 small onion, minced
- 1 packet of chopped spinach frozen, thawed and drained
- 1 can of mushrooms, drained
- 1 package (6 oz) of herb and garlic feta cheese, crumbled
- 1 package (8 oz) of grated cheddar cheese
- 1 deep uncooked pie crust

- 4 eggs, beaten
- salt and pepper to taste

Instructions

1. Preheat the oven to 190 ° C.
2. Melt the butter in a medium-sized pan over medium heat. Bake garlic and onion in butter until light brown, about 7 minutes. Stir in the spinach, mushrooms, feta cheese, and 1/2 cup of cheddar cheese. Season with salt and pepper pour the mixture into the pie crust.
3. Beat eggs and milk in a medium bowl. Season with salt and pepper. Pour into the dish of the dough and let the egg mixture mix well with the spinach mixture.
4. Bake in the preheated oven for 15 minutes. Sprinkle with remaining Cheddar cheese and cook for a further 35 to 40 minutes, until the mixture is in the middle. Let stand for 10 minutes before serving.

Macros

Per serving: 613 calories; 48.2 g fat; 23.9 g carbohydrates; 22.9 g protein; 232 mg cholesterol; 1155 mg sodium

148. Cranberry Sauce

Prep time: 10 minutes
Servings: 11
Ingredients

- 12 ounces cranberries
- 1 cup white sugar
- 1 cup of orange juice

Instruction

- In a saucepan over medium heat, dissolve the sugar in the orange juice.
- Stir in the cranberries and cook until the cranberries begin to appear (about 10 minutes). Remove from heat and put the sauce in a bowl. The cranberry sauce becomes thicker as it cools.

Macros

Per serving: 95 calories; 0.1 g fat; 24.2 g carbohydrates; 0.3 g of protein; 0 mg of cholesterol; <1 mg sodium.

149. Vegetarian Meatloaf

Prep time: 25 minutes
Servings: 8
Ingredients

- 1 bottle of barbecue sauce

- 1 package of vegetarian burgers (12 oz)
- 1 green pepper, minced
- 1/3 cup chopped onion
- 1 clove garlic
- 1/2 cup breadcrumbs
- 3 tablespoons Parmesan cheese
- 1 beaten egg
- 1/4 teaspoon dried thyme
- 1/4 c. dried basil
- 1/4 teaspoon
- Salt and pepper to taste

Instructions

1. Preheat the oven to 165 ° C (325 ° F). Grease a 5 x 9-inch light bread pan.
2. In a bowl, mix half of the barbecue sauce with the vegetarian burgers, green pepper, onion, garlic, breadcrumbs, parmesan cheese, and egg. Season with thyme, basil, parsley, salt, and pepper put in the bread pan.
3. Bake for 45 minutes in the preheated oven. Pour the rest of the barbecue sauce onto the bread and continue to cook for 15 minutes.

Macros

Per serving: 155 calories; 3.3 g of fat; 21.3 g carbohydrates; 9.6 g of protein; 25 mg cholesterol; 688 mg of sodium

150. Vegetarian Kale Soup

Prep time: 25 minutes
Servings: 8
Ingredients

- 2 tablespoons olive oil
- 1 yellow onion, minced
- 2 tablespoons chopped garlic
- 1 bunch of kale, stems removed and chopped
- 8 cups of water
- 6 cubes of vegetable broth
- 1 can of tomato cubes (15 grams)
- 6 white potatoes, peeled and diced
- 2 cans cannellini beans (drained if desired)
- 1 tablespoon of Italian herbs
- 2 tablespoons dried parsley
- pepper to taste

Instructions

1. Heat the olive oil in a large pan; cook onion and garlic until soft. Stir in kale and cook until soft, about 2 minutes.
2. Stir in water, vegetable stock, tomatoes, potatoes, beans, Italian herbs, and parsley.

3. Let the soup simmer for 25 minutes over medium heat or until the potatoes are tender. Season with salt and pepper.

Macros

Per serving: 277 calories; 4.5 g fat; 50.9 g carbohydrates; 9.6 g of protein; 0 mg of cholesterol; 372 mg of sodium.

151. Vegetarian Chili

Prep time: 15 minutes
Servings: 16
Ingredients

- 1 tablespoon vegetable oil
- 3 garlic cloves
- 1 cup chopped onion
- 1 cup chopped carrots
- 1 cup chopped green pepper
- 1 cup chopped red pepper
- 2 tablespoons chili powder
- 1 1/2 cup fresh chopped mushrooms
- 1 can of peeled whole tomatoes (28 oz) with liquid
- 1 can (15 oz) black beans, minced, not drained
- 1 can (15 oz) of red beans, not drained
- 1 can of 15 pinto beans, not drained
- 1 can of whole-grain corn, drained
- 1 tablespoon of cumin
- 1 1/2 tablespoon dried oregano
- 1 1/2 tablespoon dried basil
- 1/2 tablespoon garlic powder

Instructions

1. Heat the oil in a large saucepan over medium heat. Cook and mix the garlic, onion, and carrots in the pan until soft. Stir in the green pepper and red pepper. Season with chili powder. Continue to cook for 5 minutes or until the pepper is soft.
2. Mix the mushrooms in the pot. Stir in the tomatoes with the liquid, the black beans with the liquid, the red beans with the liquid, the pinto beans with the liquid, and the corn. Season with cumin, oregano, basil, and garlic powder. Bring to boil.
3. Lower the heat, cover, and cook for 20 minutes, stirring occasionally.

Macros

Per serving: 98 calories; 1.8 g fat; 18.5 g carbohydrates; 4.4 g of protein; 0 mg of cholesterol; 278 mg of sodium.

CHAPTER 9: BREAD & PIZZA

There are many who claim to have the "best" recipe for pizza. Preparing pizzas is an art and a science.

Bread recipes are a great way to make homemade bread. Of course, you can use a bread machine that will do the work for you, but you will miss out on the pleasure of making it yourself.

Most bread recipes are incredibly easy to follow, and baked products will delight your taste buds. Take the time to bake and see how quickly everything disappears!

152. Bread Machine Pizza Dough

Prep time: 15 minutes

Servings: 6

Ingredients

- 1 cup of beer
- 2 tablespoons butter
- 2 tablespoons sugar
- 1 teaspoon of salt
- 2 1/2 cups of all-purpose flour
- 2 1/4 teaspoons of yeast

Instructions

1. Place beer, butter, sugar, salt, flour, and yeast in a bread maker in the order recommended by the manufacturer. Select the Paste setting and press Start.
2. Remove the dough from the bread maker once the cycle is complete. Roll or press the dough to cover a prepared pizza dish. Brush lightly with olive oil. Cover and let stand for 15 minutes.
3. Preheat the oven to 200 degrees C (400 degrees F).
4. Spread the sauce and garnish on the dough. Bake until the crust is a little brown and crispy on the outside, about 24 minutes.

Macros

Per serving: 262 calories; 4.4 g fat; 46 g carbohydrates; 6.2 g of protein; 10 mg cholesterol; 418 mg of sodium

153. Grilling Dough

Prep time: 15 minutes

Servings: 12

Ingredients

- 1/2 teaspoon of salt
- 2 cups of flour
- 1/2 teaspoon white sugar
- 1 packet (0.25 oz) active dry yeast

- 1 tablespoon olive oil
- 2 tablespoons cornmeal for dusting
- 3/4 cup of hot water

Instructions

1. Mix yeast in hot water.
2. Put the flour, salt, sugar, and oil in a separate bowl. Make a well in the middle and place the yeast / warm water mixture. Mix well until you have an elastic ball. Let rise for 1 1/2 hours.
3. Flour the surface and divide 1/2 dough. Rub with cornmeal. Sprinkle with your favorite fillings.
4. Spray the grill with a cooking spray. Grill the dough for about 5 minutes or until the toppings are melted. Repeat this with the second piece of dough.

Macros

Per serving: 93 calories; 1.4 g fat; 17.3 g carbohydrates; 2.5 g of protein; 0 mg of cholesterol; 98 mg of sodium

154. Pizza Crust

Prep time: 10 minutes

Servings: 15

Ingredients

- 7/8 cup warm water
- 3/4 teaspoon salt
- 2 tablespoons olive oil
- 2 1/2 cups all-purpose flour
- 2 teaspoons white sugar
- 2 teaspoons active dry yeast

Instructions

1. Add the ingredients in the order suggested by your manufacturer. Set the bread machine to adjust the dough and start the machine.
2. Tap the dough into a rolling pan or a 12-inch greased round pizza pan. Let stand for 10

minutes. Preheat the oven to 205 ° C (400 ° F) spread the pizza sauce on the dough. Sprinkle the toppings over the sauce. Bake for 15-20 minutes or until the crust is golden brown.

Macros

Per serving: 95 calories; 2 grams of fat; 16.7 g of carbohydrates; 2.4 g of protein; 0 mg cholesterol; 117 mg of sodium.

155. Dill & Parmesan Flatbread

Prep time: 10 minutes

Servings: 12

Ingredients

- 2 cups of garbanzo flour
- 3 tablespoons freshly grated Parmesan cheese
- 2 teaspoons dill
- 1 teaspoon salt
- freshly ground black pepper to taste
- 2 cups of water, divided
- 1/4 cup of olive oil, divide

Instructions

1. Combine flour, parmesan, dill, salt, and black pepper in a bowl. Stir in 1 1/2 cups of water and 3 tablespoons of olive oil. Let the dough rest for about 30 minutes.
2. Heat up the oven to 200 degrees C (400 degrees F). Grease a large pizza dish with the rest of the olive oil.
3. Mix 1/2 cup of the remaining water in the dough, not on the prepared pizza pan.
4. Bake in the preheated oven until the top is golden brown, about 10 minutes.

Macros

Per serving: 102 calories; 5.9 g fat; 9.3 g of carbohydrates; 3.6 g of protein; 1 mg cholesterol; 215 mg of sodium.

156. Pizza Buns

Prep time: 10 minutes

Servings: 8

Ingredients

- 8 hamburger buns, divided
- 1 pound ground beef
- 1/3 cup onion, minced

- 1 (15 oz) jar pizza sauce
- 1/3 cup grated Parmesan cheese
- 2 1/4 teaspoon Italian herbs
- 1 teaspoon garlic powder
- 1/4 cup Onion powder
- 1/8 teaspoon ground crushed red pepper flakes
- 1 teaspoon bell pepper
- 2 cups grated mozzarella cheese

Instructions

1. Preheat the oven grill and place the oven rack about 6 centimeters from the heat source.
2. Place the buns on a baking sheet. Grill for about 1 minute until they are toasted. Set aside.
3. Set the oven to 350 degrees F (175 degrees C).
4. In a large frying pan over medium heat, cook and mix the minced beef until it is golden and crumbly, about 10 minutes. Drain the excess fat and stir in the onion. Cook and mix the beef mixture until the onion is transparent, about 5 minutes longer, then add the pizza sauce, parmesan cheese, Italian herbs, garlic powder, onion powder, ground red pepper flakes, and bell pepper.
5. Bring the sauce to a boil and simmer for 10 to 15 minutes to mix the flavors, stirring often.
6. Pour the beef sauce over the baking sheet and cover each loaf with about 1/4 cup grated mozzarella cheese. Put the rolls back in the oven and bake for about 10 minutes, until the cheese is bubbling and light brown.

Macros

Per serving: 341 calories; 14.4 g of fat; 29 g carbohydrates; 22.3 g of protein; 55 mg cholesterol; 787 mg of sodium.

157. Brick Oven Pizza (Brooklyn Style)

Prep time: 25 minutes
Servings: 18

Ingredients

- 1 teaspoon of active dry yeast
- 1/4 cup of warm water
- 1 cup of cold water
- 1 teaspoon of salt
- 3 cups of bread flour
- 6 oz low-mozzarella cheese, minced
- 1/2 cup of crushed canned tomatoes without salt
- 1/4 teaspoon of freshly ground black pepper
- 1/2 teaspoon dried oregano
- 3 tablespoons extra virgin olive oil
- 6 fresh basil leaves, torn

Instructions

1. Sprinkle the yeast over the warm water in a large bowl. Let stand for 5 minutes to check. Stir in salt and cold water, and then add about 1 cup of flour at a time. When the dough is thick enough to be removed from the bowl, knead it on a floured surface until smooth, about 10 minutes.
2. Divide it in two and form a tight ball. Coat the balls with olive oil and leave them in a sealed container for at least 16 hours. Use a container that is large enough to allow the dough to rise. Remove the dough from the fridge one hour before use.
3. Preheat the oven with a pizza stone on the lowest rack at 550 degrees F. Lightly dust a pizza skin with flour.
4. Use a ball of dough at a time, sprinkle the dough lightly with flour, and gradually stretch it until it is approximately 14 inches in diameter, about the size of the pizza stone. Place on the floured tin.
5. Place thin slices of mozzarella on the crust and then chop a generous amount of black pepper. Sprinkle with dried oregano. Arrange the crushed tomatoes randomly and leave empty areas. Sprinkle with olive oil.
6. Make sure the dough comes off the skin with a quick jerk. Place the tip of the skin on the back of the preheated pizza stone and remove it to leave the pizza on the stone.

7. Bake in the preheated oven for 4 to 6 minutes or until the crust starts to brown. Remove from the oven by sliding the skin under the pizza. Randomly sprinkle some basil leaves on the pizza. Cut into segments and serve.

Macros

Per serving: 145 calories; 4.7 g of fat; 19.4 g carbohydrates; 5.8 g of protein; 7 mg of cholesterol; 213 mg of sodium.

158. Valentine Pizza

Prep time: 30 minutes
Servings: 12

Ingredients

- 3 cups of bread flour
- 1 (0.25 oz) active dry yeast cover
- 1 1/4 cup of warm water
- 3 tablespoons chopped fresh rosemary
- 3 tablespoons extra virgin olive oil, divided
- 1 can of pizza sauce (14 oz)
- 3 cups grated mozzarella cheese
- 2 ripe tomatoes
- 15 slices of vegetarian pepperoni
- 1 can (2.25 oz) sliced black olives, sliced
- 1 zucchini, sliced

Instructions

1. Place the bread flour, yeast, water and 2 tablespoons of olive oil in the bread maker in the order recommended by the manufacturer. Select the Paste setting. Press Start. When the dough is ready, knead the rosemary into the dough.
2. Heat up the oven to 200 degrees C (400 degrees F).
3. Divide the dough into three servings. Shape each heart-shaped piece about 1/2 inch thick. Brush with remaining olive oil, then spread a thin layer of pizza sauce on each pizza. Sprinkle cheese over pizza sauce and arrange on top with tomatoes, zucchini, pepperoni, and sliced olives.
4. Bake for about 15 to 20 minutes or until the cheese has melted and the crust is brown.

Macros

Per serving: 261 calories; 9.1 g of fat; 31 grams of carbohydrates 13.2 g of protein; 18 mg cholesterol; 432 mg of sodium.

159. Pizza Muffins

Prep time: 20 minutes
Servings: 12
Ingredients

- 2 1/2 cups flour
- 1/2 teaspoon baking powder
- 1/2 teaspoon dried oregano
- 2 tablespoons white sugar
- 1/2 teaspoon salt
- 1 teaspoon dried basil leaves
- 3 sun-dried tomatoes, packed in oil, drained and diced
- 2 1/2 cups of cheddar cheese, grated, divided
- 4 green onions, minced
- 1 beaten egg
- 1 1/2 cup buttermilk

Instruction

1. Preheat the oven to 190 ° C. Grease the muffin cups or double them with muffin paper.
2. Combine flour, baking powder, baking powder, salt, basil, oregano and sugar in a large bowl in a large bowl. Stir until everything is well mixed. Mix tomatoes, 1.5 cups of cheese, and onions. In another bowl, whisk the egg, pick up buttermilk and stir until smooth. Place the dough halfway in the muffin pans. Sprinkle the remaining cup of cheese over the muffins.
3. Bake in the preheated oven for 15 to 20 minutes, until a toothpick in the middle of the muffin comes out clean.

Macros

Per serving: 241 calories; 10.6 g fat; 24.6 g carbohydrates; 11.5 g of protein; 47 mg of cholesterol; 429 mg of sodium.

160. Pita Pizza

Prep time: 5 minutes
Servings: 12
Ingredients

- 6 pita bread
- 1 can of tomato sauce
- 1 can (4 grams) sliced black olives, drained
- 1 ounce diced bell pepper, drained
- 2 small tomatoes, minced
- 4 oz grated mozzarella cheese
- 4 grams of blue cheese, crumbled
- 1 pinch of dried basil
- 1 pinch of dried oregano
- 1 pinch of coriander crushed

Instruction

1. Preheat the oven to 220 ° C.
2. Heat the pita bread for 1 minute or until soft in the preheated oven or microwave. Slightly spread the tomato sauce and press flat while spreading. Sprinkle with black olives, chili peppers, tomatoes, mozzarella, blue cheese, basil, oregano, and coriander.
3. Spread the pita bread on a large baking sheet and place in the preheated oven for 8 minutes or until the pita bread has reached the desired crispiness. Serve whole or in slices.

Macros

Per serving: 158 calories; 5.7 g fat; 19.5 g of carbohydrates; 7.5 g of protein; 13 mg of cholesterol; 514 mg of sodium.

161. Pub Pizza

Prep time: 10 minutes
Servings: 1
Ingredients

- 1 small (4 inches) pita bread
- 1/4 cup pizza sauce
- 4 slices cooked ham
- 1/4 cup pineapple chunks, drained
- 4 slices Monterey Jack cheese

Instructions

1. Heat up the oven to 200 degrees C (400 degrees F).
2. Place the pita bread on a small baking sheet. Cover with pizza sauce, ham and pieces of pineapple garnish with Monterey Jack cheese.
3. Bake in the preheated oven for 12 to 15 minutes, until cheese, is melted and light brown.

Macros

Per serving: 845 calories; 55.7 grams of fat; 32 grams of carbohydrates, 52.5 grams of protein; 164 mg of cholesterol; 2542 mg of sodium.

162. Alfredo Chicken Pita Pizza

Prep time: 20 minutes
Servings: 4
Ingredients

- olive oil, divided
- 6 small frozen chicken fillets, thawed and sliced
- 1 pinch of salt with garlic or to taste
- 1/4 cup of garlic hummus
- 4 pita breads
- 4 teaspoons of basil pesto
- 1/2 cup of prepared Alfredo sauce
- 1 cup of fresh chopped spinach leaves
- 1 jar of marinated artichoke hearts (drained and minced)
- 3/4 cup grated mozzarella cheese 3/4 cup crumbled feta cheese
- 1/2 cup grated Parmesan cheese
- 1/2 cup sliced fresh mushrooms

Instructions

1. Bring the oven up to 175 ° C (350 ° F).
2. Heat 1 tablespoon of olive oil in a frying pan over medium-high heat. Season the chicken with garlic salt; cook and stir the hot oil until it is no longer pink in the middle, in 5 minutes. Set aside to cool.
3. Spread 1 tablespoon of hummus on one side of each pita bread almost to the edges. Cover with layers of pesto and alfredo sauce. Sprinkle a layer of chopped spinach on the Alfredo sauce; garnish with equal Servings of chicken, artichoke hearts, feta cheese, mozzarella, parmesan cheese, and mushrooms. Sprinkle the pizzas with the remaining olive oil.
4. Bake in the preheated oven until cheese is melted and the pita bread is light brown, about 15 minutes.

Macros

Per serving: 707 calories; 38.7 grams of fat; 39.8 g carbohydrates; 50.9 g of protein; 137 mg cholesterol; 1583 mg of sodium

163. Miniature Pizzas

Prep time: 25 minutes
Servings: 20
Ingredients

- 1 pound ground beef

- 1 pound of fresh minced pork sausage
- 1 chopped onion
- 10 grams of processed American cheese, diced
- 32 grams of cocktail rye bread

Instructions

1. Bring the oven up to 175 ° C (350 ° F).
2. In large skillet, brown ground beef and sausages.
3. Mix the onion in the sausage and beef mixture and cook until done. Pour the fat from the pan. Add the melted cheese to the mixture. Keep cooking until the cheese has melted.
4. Place the slices of bread on a baking sheet and place spoons full of the mixture on each slice of bread.
5. Bake 12 to 15 minutes.

Macros

Per serving: 338 calories; 21.1 g fat; 22.9 g carbohydrates; 13.5 g of protein; 48 mg of cholesterol; 678 mg of sodium.

164. Easy Pizza with A Pinch

Prep time: 20 minutes
Servings: 8
Ingredients

- 8 hot dog buns
- 2 cups of tomato sauce
- 3 teaspoons of minced garlic
- 3 teaspoons dried Italian herbs
- 1 tbsp. Sweet pepper
- 1 tbsp. Kosher salt
- 1 teaspoon ground black pepper
- 1 pound of sweet Italian sausages
- 2 tablespoons extra virgin olive oil
- 1 cup of grated mozzarella cheese
- 1/2 cup grated Parmesan cheese
- fresh oregano sprigs (optional)
- Ground red pepper (optional)

Instructions

1. To make the sauce, mix tomato sauce, garlic, pepper, salt, and pepper in a pan over medium heat.
2. When the sauce is bubbling, place on low heat and stir. Cover and simmer for 15 minutes on low heat.
3. Crumble the Italian sausages in a pan and cook them over medium heat until they are

no longer pink, about 15 minutes. Drain on kitchen paper. Set aside.

4. Preheat the oven to 400 degrees F.
5. Combine olive oil, garlic, and 1 teaspoon in a small bowl.
6. Open the hot dog buns and place them on baking trays with aluminum foil.
7. Brush the buns with the olive oil mixture. Grill for about 5 minutes, until the edges start to brown.
8. Remove the pan from the oven and brush each sandwich with hot tomato sauce.
9. Garnish with golden Italian sausages, sliced pepperoni, mozzarella, and parmesan cheese.
10. Return the pan to the oven and bake for 5 to 10 minutes at 400 ° F or until the cheese is bubbling.
11. Serve garnished with fresh oregano leaves and chopped red pepper, if desired.

Macros

Per serving: 32 g fat; 516 calories; 31.6 g carbohydrates; 24.5 g of protein; 66 mg of cholesterol; 1887 mg of sodium

165. Pesto Pita Pizza

Prep time: 15 minutes
Servings: 4
Ingredients

- 4 pita bread rounds
- 1/2 cup pesto
- 2 tomatoes, sliced
- 1 (4 oz) container crumbled feta cheese

Instructions

1. Preheat oven to 375 degrees F (190 degrees C). Arrange pita bread on a baking sheet.
2. Bake in the preheated oven until pita is lightly toasted, about 4 minutes.
3. Spread pesto evenly over toasted pita bread and arrange tomato slices in a single layer. Top with feta cheese.
4. Continue baking until feta cheese is browned, and pita bread is crisp, about 11 minutes more.

Macros

Per serving: 378 calories; 20.9 g fat; 33.4 g carbohydrates; 14.7 g protein; 35 mg cholesterol; 824 mg sodium

166. Veggie Pita Pizza

Prep time: 5 minutes
Servings: 1
Ingredients

- 1 round pita bread
- 1 teaspoon of olive oil
- 3 tablespoons of pizza sauce
- 1/2 cup grated mozzarella cheese
- 1/4 cup sliced Cremini mushrooms
- 1/8 teaspoon salt with garlic

Instructions

1. Preheat the grill on medium heat.
2. Spread a side of the pita with olive oil and pizza sauce. Garnish with cheese and mushrooms and season with garlic salt.
3. Lightly grease the grill. Place the pita pizza on the grill, cover, and cook until the cheese has completely melted about 5 minutes.

Macros

Per serving: 405 calories; 18 g fat; 39.9 g carbohydrates; 19.7 g of protein; 44 mg cholesterol; 1156 mg of sodium.

167. Mini Pizzas with Arugula & Hummus

Prep time: 10 minutes
Servings: 1
Ingredients

- 2 tablespoons hummus
- 1 naan bread
- 1 cup of arugula
- 1 date, pitted and chopped
- 2 teaspoons pumpkin seeds
- 1 teaspoon balsamic vinegar

Instructions

1. Spread the hummus on naan bread; garnish with arugula, date, and pumpkin seeds.
2. Sprinkle balsamic vinegar on pizza.

Macros

Per serving: 350 calories; 8.5 g fat; 56.8 g of carbohydrates; 14.4 g of protein; 10 mg cholesterol; 424 mg of sodium.

168. Grilled Buffalo Chicken Pizza

Prep time: 15 minutes
Servings: 2
Ingredients

- 1 boneless chicken fillet
- 2 pinches of steak herbs
- 2 tablespoons hot pepper sauce
- 2 pieces of naan tandoori bread
- 1 teaspoon of olive oil
- ½ cup of blue cheese dressing
- 2 tablespoons diced red onion
- 8 grams of grated cheddar cheese
- ½ cup of grated iceberg lettuce
- 1 Roma tomato, seeded and minced

Instructions

1. Season the chicken fillet with Montreal Steak Seasoning. Put the chicken in a resealable plastic bag and pour 1/3 cup of hot pepper sauce into the bag. Close the bag and rub the hot sauce into the chicken. Place the bag in the refrigerator and marinate for 12 hours.
2. Preheat an outside grill over medium heat and lightly oil the grill.
3. Remove the chicken from the bag and discard the marinade. Cook the chicken on the preheated grill until it is no longer pink in the middle, and the juice is clear, 5 to 7 minutes on each side. An instant-read thermometer in the center must indicate at least 165 ° F (74 ° C). Place the chicken on a cutting board and let it sit for 5 to 10 minutes.
4. Cut the chilled chicken into bite-sized pieces. Mix chicken and remaining hot sauce in a bowl.
5. Brush every naan with olive oil; bake on the grill until golden brown and grilled on one side for 3 to 5 minutes. Reduce the heat to low and medium and place the pieces of toasted bread on a baking sheet. Spread blue cheese vinaigrette on the grilled side of each naan. Garnish each with diced chicken and red onion. Sprinkle with cheddar cheese.
6. Place the Naan on the grill and cook until the cheese has melted and the bottom is grilled and golden brown, another 5 to 10 minutes. Remove from the grill, cut into pieces and garnish with lettuce and tomato.

Macros
Per serving: 1170 calories; 78 g total fat; 204 mg of cholesterol; 3328 mg of sodium. 53.7 g of carbohydrates; 65.5 g of protein;

169. Reuben Pizza

Prep time: 25 minutes
Servings: 8
Ingredients

- 1 frozen whole meal bread, thawed
- 1/2 cup thousand island vinaigrette
- 2 cups of grated Swiss cheese
- 6 grams of salted beef, sliced
- 1 cup sauerkraut, rinsed and drained
- 1/2 teaspoon cumin seeds
- 1/4 cup chopped dill pickles (optional)

Instructions

1. Preheat the oven to 190° C. Grease a large pizza dish. Roll bread dough on a lightly floured surface into a large circle about 14 inches in diameter. Transfer to the prepared pizza dish. Build the edges and pierce the center with a fork so that it does not form a dome during cooking.
2. Bake in the preheated oven for 20 to 25 minutes or until golden brown.
3. Spread half the vinaigrette over the hot crust. Sprinkle with half the Swiss cheese. Place the corned beef on the cheese and pour the rest of the vinaigrette. Cover with sauerkraut and remaining Swiss cheese. Sprinkle with cumin seeds.
4. Bake for another 10 minutes in the preheated oven until the cheese has melted and the toppings are well heated. Sprinkle with chopped pickle. Let stand for 5 minutes before cutting.

Macros
Per serving: 207 calories; 15.4 grams of fat; 6.4 g carbohydrates; 11.6 g of protein; 44 mg cholesterol; 698 mg of sodium

170. White Pizza

Prep time: 10 minutes
Servings: 8
Ingredients

- 1 (12-inch) pre-baked thin pizza crust
- 2 tablespoons extra-virgin olive oil, divided
- 3 cups shredded mozzarella cheese
- 8 cloves garlic, quartered

Instructions

1. Preheat the oven to 230 ° C.
2. 2. Place the pizza crust on a baking sheet and pour 1 spoonful of olive oil in. Add the mozzarella cheese over the crust evenly, and garnish with garlic pieces.
3. Bake in the preheated oven until cheese bubbles and turns brown for about 15 minutes. Sprinkle with a little more olive oil and cut into quarters to serve.

Macros

Per serving: 292 calories; 13.1 g fat; 27.2 g carbohydrates; 17.5 g of protein; 32 mg of cholesterol; 553 mg of sodium.

CHAPTER 10: SNACKS

Everybody needs or craves a snack through the day and according to dietitians, they recommend that rather than having 3 heavy meals, one should split this into six smaller meals to maintain their health, lose weight and boost metabolism. In other words, enjoy a smaller breakfast , lunch and dinner to incorporate 3 smaller, healthier snacks in between so the body never feels hungry and your metabolism stays on track.

Here are some simple snack recipes:

171. Guacamole

Prep time: 10 minutes

Servings: 4

Ingredients

- 3 avocados - peeled, seeded and mashed
- 1 lime, juiced
- 1 teaspoon salt
- 1/2 cup diced onion
- 3 tablespoons chopped fresh coriander
- 2 Roma tomatoes, diced
- 1 teaspoon chopped garlic
- 1 pinch of ground cayenne pepper (optional)

Instructions

1. Puree avocados, lime juice, and salt in a medium bowl.
2. Stir in the onion, coriander, tomatoes, and garlic. Stir in the cayenne pepper.

Macros

Per serving: 262 calories; 22.2 g fat; 18 grams of carbohydrates 3.7 g of protein; 0 mg of cholesterol; 596 mg of sodium

172. Sugar-coated Pecans

Prep time: 15 minutes

Servings: 12

Ingredients

- 1 egg white
- 1 tablespoon water
- 1 pound pecan halves
- 1 cup white sugar
- 3/4 teaspoon salt
- 1/2 teaspoon ground cinnamon

Instructions

1. Preheat the oven to 120 ° C (250 ° F). Grease a baking tray.
2. In a bowl, whisk the egg whites and water until frothy. Combine the sugar, salt, and cinnamon in another bowl.

3. Add the pecans to the egg whites and stir to cover the nuts. Remove the nuts and mix them with the sugar until well covered. Spread the nuts on the prepared baking sheet.
4. Bake for 1 hour at 250 ° F (120 ° C). Stir every 15 minutes.

Macros

Per serving: 328 calories; 27.2 g fat; 22 grams of carbohydrates 3.8 g of protein; 0 mg of cholesterol; 150 mg of sodium

173. Southwestern Egg Rolls

Prep time: 20 minutes

Servings: 5

Ingredients

- 2 tablespoons vegetable oil
- 1/2 chicken fillet, skinless
- 2 tablespoons chopped green onion
- 2 tablespoons chopped red pepper
- 1/3 cup frozen corn kernels
- 1/4 cup black rinsed and drained beans
- 2 tsp chopped frozen spinach, thawed and drained
- 2 tablespoons diced jalapeño peppers
- 1/2 tablespoon chopped fresh parsley
- 1/2 c. ground cumin
- 1/2 teaspoon chili powder
- 1/3 teaspoon salt
- 1 pinch of ground cayenne pepper
- 3/4 cup of grated Monterey Jack cheese
- 5 flour tortillas (6 inches)
- 1 liter of oil for frying

Instructions

1. Rub 1 tablespoon of vegetable oil on the chicken fillet. Cook the chicken in a medium-sized saucepan over medium heat for about 5 minutes per side until the meat is no longer

pink and the juice is clear. Remove from heat and set aside.

2. Heat 1 tablespoon of remaining vegetable oil in a medium-sized saucepan over medium heat. Stir in the green onion and red pepper. Boil and stir for 5 minutes, until soft.
3. Cut the diced chicken and mix in the pan with the onion and red pepper. Mix corn, black beans, spinach, jalapeño pepper, parsley, cumin, chili powder, salt, and cayenne pepper. Boil and stir for 5 minutes, until everything is well mixed and soft. Remove from heat and stir in Monterey Jack cheese until it melts.
4. Wrap the tortillas with slightly damp cloth — microwave at maximum power, about 1 minute, or until it is hot and malleable.
5. Pour equal amounts of the mixture into each tortilla. Fold the ends of the tortillas and wrap the mixture well. Safe with toothpicks. Arrange in a medium-sized dish, cover with plastic, and place in the freezer. Freeze for at least 4 hours.
6. Heat the oil in a deep frying pan to 190° C for frying. Bake frozen stuffed tortillas for 10 minutes or until golden brown. Drain on paper towels before serving.

Macros

Per serving: 419 calories; 31.2 g fat; 21.8 g of carbohydrates; 13.6 g of protein; 29 mg of cholesterol; 575 mg of sodium

174. Annie's Salsa Chips with Fruit & Cinnamon

Prep time: 15 minutes

Servings: 10

Ingredients

- 2 Golden Delicious apples - peeled, seeded and diced
- 8 grams of raspberry
- 2 kiwis, peeled and diced
- 1 pound of strawberries
- 2 tablespoons of white sugar
- 1 tablespoon of brown sugar
- 3 tablespoons canned fruit
- flour cooking aerosol
- flour tortillas
- 2 tablespoons cinnamon sugar

Instructions

1. Combine kiwi, Golden Delicious apples, raspberries, strawberries, white sugar, brown sugar, and canned fruit in a large bowl. Cover and put in the fridge for at least 15 minutes.
2. Bring the oven up to 175 ° C (350 ° F).
3. Cover one side of each flour tortilla with a cooking spray. Cut into segments and place them in one layer on a large baking sheet. Sprinkle the quarters with the desired amount of cinnamon sugar. Spray again with cooking spray.
4. Bake in the preheated oven for 8 to 10 minutes. Repeat this with the other tortilla quarters. Cool for approximately 15 minutes. Serve with a mixture of fresh fruit.

Macros

Per serving: 312 calories; 5.9 g fat; 59 grams of carbohydrates 6.8 g of protein; 0 mg of cholesterol; 462 mg of sodium.

175. Boneless Buffalo Wings

Prep time: 10 minutes

Servings: 3

Ingredients

- frying oil
- 1 cup unbleached flour
- 2 teaspoons of salt
- 1/2 teaspoon ground black pepper
- 1/2 teaspoon cayenne pepper
- 1/4 teaspoon garlic powder
- 1/2 teaspoon bell pepper
- 1 egg
- 1 cup of milk
- 3 boneless chicken fillets, skinless, cut into 1/2 inch strips
- 1/4 cup hot pepper sauce
- 1 tablespoon butter

Instructions

1. Heat the oil in a frying pan or large saucepan.
2. Mix the flour, salt, black pepper, cayenne pepper, garlic powder, and bell pepper in a large bowl. Beat the egg and milk in a small bowl. Dip each piece of chicken in the egg mixture and then roll it into the flour mixture. Repeat the process so that each

piece of chicken is doubled. Cool the breaded chicken for 20 minutes.

3. Fry chicken in hot oil, in batches. Cook until the outside is well browned and the juice is clear, 5 to 6 minutes per batch.
4. Mix the hot sauce and butter in a small bowl. Heat the sauce in the microwave on high to melt, 20 to 30 seconds. Pour the sauce over the cooked chicken; mix well.

Macros

Per serving: 710 calories 46.9 g fat; 43.7 g of carbohydrates; 28 g of protein; 136 mg of cholesterol; 2334 mg of sodium.

176. Jalapeño Popper Spread

Prep time: 10 minutes

Servings: 32

Ingredients

- 2 packets of cream cheese, softened
- 1 cup mayonnaise
- 1 (4-gram) can chopped green peppers, drained
- 2 grams diced jalapeño peppers, canned, drained
- 1 cup grated Parmesan cheese

Instructions

1. In a large bowl, mix cream cheese and mayonnaise until smooth. Stir the bell peppers and jalapeño peppers.
2. Pour the mixture into a microwave oven and sprinkle with Parmesan cheese.
3. Microwave on maximum power, about 3 minutes.

Macros

Per serving: 110 calories; 11.1 grams of fat; 1 g of carbohydrates; 2.1 g of protein; 20 mg of cholesterol; 189 mg of sodium.

177. Brown Sugar Smokies

Prep time: 10 minutes

Servings: 12

Ingredients

- 1 pound bacon
- 1 (16 ounces) package little smokie sausages
- 1 cup brown sugar, or to taste

Instructions

1. Bring the oven up to 175 ° C (350 ° F).
2. Cut the bacon in three and wrap each strip around a little sausage. Place sausages wrapped on wooden skewers, several to one place the kebabs on a baking sheet and sprinkle generously with brown sugar.
3. Bake until the bacon is crispy, and the brown sugar has melted.

Macros

Per serving: 356 calories; 27.2 g fat; 18.9 g of carbohydrates; 9 g of protein; 49 mg cholesterol; 696 mg of sodium.

178. Pita Chips

Prep time: 10 minutes

Servings: 24

Ingredients

- 12 slices of pita bread
- 1/2 cup of olive oil
- 1/2 teaspoon ground black pepper
- 1 teaspoon garlic salt
- 1/2 teaspoon dried basil
- 1 teaspoon dried chervil

Instructions

1. Preheat the oven to 200 degrees C (400 degrees F).
2. Cut each pita bread into 8 triangles. Place the triangles on the baking sheet.
3. Combine oil, pepper, salt, basil, and chervil in a small bowl. Brush each triangle with the oil mixture.
4. Bake in the preheated oven for about 7 minutes or until light brown and crispy.

Macros

Per serving: 125 calories; 5.3 g fat; 17.7 g of carbohydrates; 3.2 g of protein; 0 mg of cholesterol; 246 mg of sodium

179. Hot Spinach, Artichoke & Chili Dip

Prep time: 10 minutes

Servings: 10

Ingredients

- 2 (8 oz) packages of cream cheese, softened
- 1/2 cup of mayonnaise
- 1 can (4.5 oz) chopped green pepper, drained
- 1 cup of freshly grated Parmesan cheese
- 1 jar (12 oz) marinated artichoke hearts, drained and chopped
- 1/4 cup canned chopped jalapeño peppers, drained
- 1 can of chopped spinach frozen, thawed and drained

Instructions

1. Bring the oven up to 175 ° C (350 ° F).
2. Mix the cream cheese and mayonnaise in a bowl. Stir the green peppers, parmesan cheese, artichokes, peppers, and spinach. Pour the mixture into a baking dish.
3. Bake in the preheated oven until light brown, about 30 minutes.

Macros

Per serving: 314 calories; 28.8 g of fat; 7.8 grams of carbohydrates; 9 g of protein; 60 mg cholesterol; 682 mg of sodium.

180. Fruit Dip

Prep time: 5 minutes

Servings: 12

Ingredients
- 1 (8-oz) package cream cheese, softened
- 1 (7-oz) jar marshmallow creme

Instruction

1. Use an electric mixer to combine the cream cheese and marshmallow
2. Beat until everything is well mixed.

Macros

Per serving: 118 calories; 6.6 g fat; 13.4 g carbohydrates; 1.5 g of protein; 21 mg of cholesterol; 68 mg of sodium.

181. Spooky Spider Snacks

Prep time: 15 minutes

Servings: 10

Ingredients

- 20 buttery round crackers
- 5 tablespoons pressurized canned Cheddar cheese spread
- 60 pretzel sticks
- 20 raisins

Instructions

1. Spread 10 salted crackers evenly with about 1/2 tablespoon of spreadable cheese; cover each cookie with another to make sandwiches.
2. Stick 6 pretzel sticks in the cheese, 3 on each side, to obtain 6 legs. Put two dots of cheese on the sandwich and glue two grape eyes on each snack.

Macros

Per serving: 128 calories; 3.9 g fat; 19.7 g of carbohydrates; 3.1 g of protein; 6 mg cholesterol; 697 mg of sodium.

182. Banana & Tortilla Snacks

Prep time: 5 minutes

Servings: 1

Ingredients

- 1 flour tortilla (6 inches)
- 2 tablespoons peanut butter
- 1 tablespoon honey
- 1 banana
- 2 tablespoons raisins

Instructions

- Lay the tortilla flat. Spread peanut butter and honey on the tortilla. Place the banana in the middle and sprinkle the raisins. Wrap and serve.

Macros

Per serving: 520 calories; 19.3 grams of fat; 82.9 g carbohydrates; 12.8 g of protein; 0 mg of cholesterol; 357 mg of sodium.

183. Wonton Snacks

Prep time: 20 minutes

Servings: 48

Ingredients

- 2 pounds of ground pork
- 2 stalks of celery
- 2 carrots
- 2 cloves of garlic
- 1 small onion
- 1 (8-gram) can water chestnuts
- 1/2 cup of Thai peanut sauce prepared
- 1 package (14-oz) wonton wraps

Instructions

1. Finely chop celery, carrots, garlic, onion and water chestnuts in a food processor. Parts must be small and fairly uniform, but not liquid.
2. Mix ground pork and chopped vegetables in a large frying pan. Cook over medium heat until the vegetables are soft and the pork is no longer pink. Turn up the heat and let the moisture evaporate, then add the peanut sauce and cook for another 5 minutes before you remove it from the heat.
3. While cooking the pork mixture, Bring the oven up to 175 ° C (350 ° F). Press a wonton wrap into each cup of a mini muffin pan, with flared edges on the sides. Place a spoonful of the meat mixture in each cup.
4. Bake in the preheated oven for about 12 minutes or until the outer envelopes are crispy and golden brown.

Macros

Per serving: 86 calories 4.8 g fat; 6.1 g of carbohydrates; 4.4 g of protein; 14 mg of cholesterol; 67 mg of sodium.

184. Sesame Stick Snacks

Prep time: 15 minutes
Servings: 10

Ingredients

- 2 cups biscuit baking mix
- 2/3 cup heavy cream
- 1/4 cup butter, melted
- 1 1/2 tablespoons sesame seeds

Instructions

1. Preheat the oven to 220 ° C. Lightly grease 2 baking trays.
2. Mix the dough mixture and the cream; mix for 30 seconds. Turn the dough on a lightly floured surface and knead 10 times. Roll the dough into a 5 x 10-inch rectangle. Cut the dough into 1/2 inch wide strips.
3. Place the strips on prepared baking trays. Brush the strips with melted butter and sprinkle with sesame seeds.
4. Bake in the preheated oven for 15 minutes, until golden brown.

Macros

Per serving: 201 calories; 14.8 g of fat; 15.6 g carbohydrates; 2.3 g of protein; 34 mg cholesterol; 341 mg of sodium.

185. Shawn's Study Snacks

Prep time: 10 minutes
Servings: 60

Ingredients

- 3 bananas, pureed
- 3/4 cup butter
- 1 egg
- 1 cup of white sugar
- 1/4 cup of packaged brown sugar
- 1 teaspoon baking powder
- 2 1/2 cups flour
- 1/4 teaspoon ground nutmeg
- 1/2 teaspoon ground cinnamon
- 1 1/2 cups oatmeal
- 3/4 cup chopped walnuts
- 1/2 cup raisins (optional)

Instructions

1. Bring the oven up to 175 ° C (350 ° F).
2. Mix in order, making sure the butter or margarine is well absorbed. More flour can be added if needed.
3. Spoon soup on a greased baking sheet. Bake for 10 minutes or until the edges are light brown.

Macros

Per serving: 84 calories; 3.6 g of fat; 12.2 g carbohydrates; 1.3 g of protein; 9 mg cholesterol; 39 mg of sodium.

CHAPTER 11: DESSERTS & FRUIT

A lovely dinner doesn't feel complete until dessert is served. Desserts should always compliment the menu. Our taste buds focus on sweet, sour, and salty. If you prepared a menu that includes sweet and sour, you'd want to offer a less complex dessert.

For meals that are standard meat and potatoes, your menu's theme is a good guide. With beef or chicken entrees, the best dessert recipes may be rice pudding or apple pie. Try adding coconut to your rice pudding and top with orange slices sautéed in brown sugar. Serve apple pie with a slice of really great cheddar cheese for ultra-sophisticated simplicity. Or, try glazing it with apricot preserves and then broiling until the top turns slightly bubbly.

Fruits are not only nutritious but naturally tasty too, hence why they are refered to as nature's dessert that add colour to any dull meal. Like anything else cooked on the grill, fruits become juicier and more delicious when smoked.

Try these healthy sweet desserts!

186. Chocolate Ganache

Prep time: 10 minutes
Servings: 16
Ingredients

- 9 ounces bittersweet chocolate, chopped
- 1 cup heavy cream
- 1 tablespoon dark rum (optional)

Instructions

1. Place the chocolate in a medium bowl. Heat the cream in a small saucepan over medium heat.
2. Bring to a boil. When the cream has reached a boiling point, pour the chopped chocolate over it and beat until smooth. Stir the rum if desired.
3. Allow the ganache to cool slightly before you pour it on a cake. Start in the middle of the cake and work outside. For a fluffy icing or chocolate filling, let it cool until thick and beat with a whisk until light and fluffy.

Macros

Per serving: 142 calories; 10.8 g fat; 9.4 g of carbohydrates; 1.4 g of protein; 21 mg of cholesterol; 6 mg of sodium

187. Chocolate Covered Strawberries

Prep time: 15 minutes
Servings: 24
Ingredients

- 16 ounces milk chocolate chips
- 2 tablespoons shortening
- 1 pound fresh strawberries with leaves

Instructions

1. In a bain-marie, melt chocolate and shortening, occasionally stirring until smooth. Pierce the tops of the strawberries with toothpicks and immerse them in the chocolate mixture.
2. Turn the strawberries and put the toothpick in Styrofoam so that the chocolate cools.

Macros

Per serving: 115 calories; 7.3 g of fat; 12.7 g of carbohydrates; 1.4 g of protein; 6 mg cholesterol; 31 mg of sodium

188. Strawberry Angel Food Dessert

Prep time: 15 minutes
Servings: 18
Ingredients

- 1 angel cake (10 inches)
- 2 packages of softened cream cheese
- 1 cup of white sugar
- 1 container (8 oz) of frozen fluff, thawed
- 1 liter of fresh strawberries, sliced
- 1 jar of strawberry icing

Instructions

1. Crumble the cake in a 9 x 13-inch dish.
2. Beat the cream cheese and sugar in a medium bowl until the mixture is light and fluffy. Stir in the whipped topping. Crush the cake with your hands, and spread the cream cheese mixture over the cake.
3. Combine the strawberries and the frosting in a bowl until the strawberries are well

covered. Spread over the layer of cream cheese. Cool until ready to serve.

Macros

Per serving: 261 calories; 11 g of fat; 36.3 g carbohydrates; 3.2 g of protein; 27 mg cholesterol; 242 mg of sodium

189. Fruit Pizza

Prep time: 30 minutes

Servings: 8

Ingredients

- 1 (18-oz) package sugar cookie dough
- 1 (8-oz) package cream cheese, softened
- 1 (8-oz) frozen filling, defrosted
- 2 cups of freshly cut strawberries
- 1/2 cup of white sugar
- 1 pinch of salt
- 1 tablespoon corn flour
- 2 tablespoons lemon juice
- 1/2 cup orange juice
- 1/4 cup water
- 1/2 teaspoon orange zest

Instructions

1. Bring the oven up to 175 ° C (350 ° F). Slice the cookie dough then place it on a greased pizza pan. Press the dough flat into the mold. Bake for 10 to 12 minutes. Let cool.
2. Soften the cream cheese in a large bowl and then stir in the whipped topping. Spread over the cooled crust.
3. Start with strawberries cut in half. Place them in a circle around the outer edge. Continue with the fruit of your choice by going to the center. If you use bananas, immerse them in lemon juice. Then make a sauce with a spoon on the fruit.
4. Combine sugar, salt, corn flour, orange juice, lemon juice, and water in a pan. Boil and stir over medium heat. Bring to a boil and cook for 1 or 2 minutes until thick. Remove from heat and add the grated orange zest. Place on the fruit.
5. Allow to cool for two hours, cut into quarters, and serve.

Macros

Per serving: 535 calories; 30 g fat; 62.9 g carbohydrates; 5.5 g of protein; 49 mg cholesterol; 357 mg of sodium

190. Bananas Foster

Prep time: 5 minutes

Servings: 4

Ingredients

- 2/3 cup dark brown sugar
- 1/4 cup butter
- 3 1/2 tablespoons rum
- 1 1/2 teaspoons vanilla extract
- 1/2 teaspoon of ground cinnamon
- 3 bananas, peeled and cut lengthwise and broad
- 1/4 cup coarsely chopped nuts
- vanilla ice cream

Instructions

1. Melt the butter in a deep frying pan over medium heat. Stir in sugar, rum, vanilla, and cinnamon.
2. When the mixture starts to bubble, place the bananas and nuts in the pan. Bake until the bananas are hot, 1 to 2 minutes. Serve immediately with vanilla ice cream.

Macros

Per serving: 534 calories; 23.8 g of fat; 73.2 g carbohydrates; 4.6 g of protein; 60 mg cholesterol; 146 mg of sodium.

191. Cranberry Orange Cookies

Prep time: 20 minutes

Servings: 48

Ingredients

3. 1 cup of soft butter
4. 1 cup of white sugar
5. 1/2 cup brown sugar
6. 1 egg
7. 1 teaspoon grated orange peel
8. 2 tablespoons orange juice
9. 2 1/2 cups flour
10. 1/2 teaspoon baking powder
11. 1/2 teaspoon salt
12. 2 cups chopped cranberries
13. 1/2 cup chopped walnuts (optional)

Icing:

14. 1/2 teaspoon grated orange peel
15. 3 tablespoons orange juice
16. 1 ½ cup confectioner's sugar

Instructions

1. Preheat the oven to 190 ° C.
2. Combine butter, white sugar, and brown sugar in a large bowl until smooth. Beat the egg until everything is well mixed. Mix 1 teaspoon of orange zest and 2 tablespoons of orange juice. Mix the flour, baking powder, and salt; stir in the orange mixture.
3. Mix the cranberries and, if used, the nuts until well distributed. Place the dough with a spoon on ungreased baking trays. The cookies must be placed at least 2 inches apart.
4. Bake in the preheated oven for 12 to 14 minutes, until the edges are golden brown. Cool on racks.
5. In a small bowl, mix icing ingredients. Spread over cooled cookies.

Macros

Per serving: 110 calories; 4.8 g fat; 16.2 g carbohydrates; 1.1 g of protein; 14 mg of cholesterol; 67 mg of sodium.

192. Key Lime Pie

Prep time: 15 minutes
Servings: 8
Ingredients

- 1 (9-inch) prepared graham cracker crust
- 3 cups of sweetened condensed milk
- 1/2 cup sour cream
- 3/4 cup lime juice
- 1 tablespoon grated lime zest

Instructions

1. Bring the oven up to 175 ° C (350 ° F).
2. Combine the condensed milk, sour cream, lime juice, and lime zest in a medium bowl. Mix well and rush into the graham cracker crust.
3. Bake in the preheated oven for 5 to 8 minutes until small hole bubbles burst on the surface of the cake.
4. Cool the cake well before serving. Decorate with lime slices and whipped cream if desired.

Macros

Per serving: 553 calories, 20.5 grams of fat; 84.7 g carbohydrates; 10.9 g of protein; 45 mg cholesterol; 324 mg of sodium

193. Rhubarb Strawberry Crunch

Prep time: 15 minutes
Servings: 18
Ingredients

- 1 cup of white sugar
- 3 tablespoons all-purpose flour
- 3 cups of fresh strawberries, sliced
- 3 cups of rhubarb, cut into cubes
- 1 1/2 cup flour
- 1 cup packed brown sugar
- 1 cup butter
- 1 cup oatmeal

Instructions

1. Preheat the oven to 190 ° C.
2. Combine white sugar, 3 tablespoons flour, strawberries and rhubarb in a large bowl. Place the mixture in a 9 x 13-inch baking dish.
3. Mix 1 1/2 cups of flour, brown sugar, butter, and oats until a crumbly texture is obtained. You may want to use a blender for this. Crumble the mixture of rhubarb and strawberry.
4. Bake in the preheated oven for 45 minutes or until crispy and light brown.

Macros

Per serving: 253 calories; 10.8 g fat; 38.1 g carbohydrates; 2.3 g of protein; 27 mg cholesterol; 78 mg of sodium.

194. Chocolate Chip Banana Dessert

Prep time: 20 minutes
Servings: 24
Ingredients

- 2/3 cup white sugar
- 3/4 cup butter
- 2/3 cup brown sugar
- 1 egg, beaten slightly
- 1 teaspoon vanilla extract
- 1 cup of banana puree
- 1 3/4 cup flour
- 2 teaspoons baking powder
- 1/2 teaspoon of salt
- 1 cup of semi-sweet chocolate chips

Instructions

1. Bring the oven up to 175 ° C (350 ° F). Grease and bake a 10 x 15-inch baking pan.
2. Beat the butter, white sugar, and brown sugar in a large bowl until light. Beat the egg and vanilla. Fold in the banana puree: mix baking powder, flour, and salt in another bowl. Stir the flour mixture into the butter mixture. Stir in the chocolate chips. Spread in the prepared pan.
3. Bake in the preheated oven for 20 minutes until the mixture is tender. Cool before cutting into squares.

Macros

Per serving: 174 calories; 8.2 g fat; 25.2 g carbohydrates; 1.7 g of protein; 23 mg of cholesterol; 125 mg of sodium.

195. Apple Pie Filling

Prep time: 20 minutes

Servings: 40

Ingredients

- 18 cups chopped apples
- 3 tablespoons lemon juice
- 10 cups of water
- 4 1/2 cups of white sugar
- 1 cup corn flour
- 2 teaspoons of ground cinnamon
- 1 teaspoon of salt
- 1/4 teaspoon ground nutmeg

Instructions

1. Mix apples with lemon juice in a large bowl and set aside. Pour the water in a Dutch oven over medium heat. Combine sugar, corn flour, cinnamon, salt, and nutmeg in a bowl. Add to water, mix well, and bring to a boil. Cook for 2 minutes with continuous stirring.
2. Add the apples and bring to a boil again. Lower the heat, cover, and simmer until the apples are soft for about 6 to 8 minutes. Allow cooling for 30 minutes.
3. Pour into five freezer containers and leave 1/2 inch of free space. Cool to room temperature.
4. Seal and freeze. It can be stored for up to 12 months.

Macros

Per serving: 129 calories; 0.1 g fat; 33.4 g carbohydrates; 0.2 g of protein; 0 mg of cholesterol; 61 mg of sodium.

196. Ice Cream Sandwich Dessert

Prep time: 20 minutes

Servings: 12

Ingredients

- 22 ice cream sandwiches
- Frozen whipped topping in 16 oz container, thawed
- 1 jar (12 oz) Caramel ice cream
- 1 1/2 cups of salted peanuts

Instructions

1. Cut a sandwich with ice in two. Place a whole sandwich and a half sandwich on a short side of a 9 x 13-inch baking dish. Repeat this until the bottom is covered, alternate the full sandwich, and the half sandwich.
2. Spread half of the whipped topping. Pour the caramel over it. Sprinkle with half the peanuts. Repeat the layers with the rest of the ice cream sandwiches, whipped cream, and peanuts.
3. Seal and place into freezer for up to 2 months. Once removed from the freezer, leave to thaw for 20 minutes before serving.

Macros

Per serving: 559 calories 28.8 g fat; 70.9 g carbohydrates; 10 g of protein; 37 mg of cholesterol; 322 mg of sodium.

197. Cranberry and Pistachio Biscotti

Prep time: 15 minutes

Servings: 36

Ingredients

- 1/4 cup light olive oil
- 3/4 cup white sugar
- 2 teaspoons vanilla extract
- 1/2 teaspoon almond extract
- 2 eggs
- 1 3/4 cup all-purpose flour
- 1/4 teaspoon salt
- 1 teaspoon baking powder
- 1/2 cup dried cranberries
- 1 1/2 cup pistachio nuts

Instructions

1. Preheat the oven to 150 ° C (300 ° F).
2. Combine the oil and sugar in a large bowl until a homogeneous mixture is obtained. Stir in the vanilla and almond extract and add the eggs. Combine flour, salt, and baking powder; gradually add to the egg mixture — mix cranberries and nuts by hand.
3. Divide the dough in half — form two 12 x 2-inch logs on a parchment baking sheet. The dough can be sticky, wet hands with cold water to make it easier to handle the dough.
4. Bake in the preheated oven for 35 minutes or until the blocks are golden brown. Remove from the oven and let cool for 10 minutes. Reduce oven heat to 275 degrees F (135 degrees C).
5. Cut diagonally into 3/4 inch thick slices. Place on the sides on the baking sheet covered with parchment — Bake for about 8 to 10 minutes or until dry; cool.

Macros

Per serving: 92 calories; 4.3 g fat; 11.7 g of carbohydrates; 2.1 g of protein; 10 mg cholesterol; 55 mg of sodium.

198. Cream Puff Dessert

Prep time: 20 minutes
Servings: 12
Ingredients
PUFF

- 1 cup water
- 1/2 cup butter
- 1 cup all-purpose flour
- 4 eggs

FILLING

- 1 (8-oz) package cream cheese, softened
- 3 1/2 cups cold milk
- 2 (4-oz) packages instant chocolate pudding mix

TOPPING

- 1 (8-oz) package frozen whipped cream topping, thawed
- 1/4 cup topping with milk chocolate flavor
- 1/4 cup caramel filling
- 1/3 cup almond flakes

Instructions

1. Preheat the oven to 200 degrees C (400 degrees F). Grease a 9 x 13-inch baking dish.

2. Melt the butter in the water in a medium-sized pan over medium heat. Pour the flour in one go and mix vigorously until the mixture forms a ball. Remove from heat and let stand for 5 minutes. Beat the eggs one by one until they are smooth and shiny. Spread in the prepared pan.
3. Bake in the preheated oven for 30 to 35 minutes, until puffed and browned. Cool completely on a rack.
4. While the puff pastry cools, mix the cream cheese mixture, the milk, and the pudding. Spread over the cooled puff pastry. Cool for 20 minutes.
5. Spread whipped cream on cooled topping and sprinkle with chocolate and caramel sauce. Sprinkle with almonds. Freeze 1 hour before serving.

Macros

Per serving: 355 calories; 22.3 g of fat; 29.2 g carbohydrates; 8.7 g of protein; 110 mg of cholesterol; 243 mg of sodium.

199. Fresh Peach Dessert

Prep time: 30 minutes
Servings: 15
Ingredients

- 16 whole graham crackers, crushed
- 3/4 cup melted butter
- 1/2 cup white sugar
- 4 1/2 cups of miniature marshmallows
- 1/4 cup of milk
- 1 pint of heavy cream
- 1/3 cup of white sugar
- 6 large fresh peaches - peeled, seeded and sliced

Instructions

1. In a bowl, mix the crumbs from the graham cracker, melted butter, and 1/2 cup of sugar. Mix until a homogeneous mixture is obtained, save 1/4 cup of the mixture for filling. Squeeze the rest of the mixture into the bottom of a 9 x 13-inch baking dish.
2. Heat marshmallows and milk in a large pan over low heat and stir until marshmallows are completely melted. Remove from heat and let cool.
3. Beat the cream in a large bowl until soft peaks occur. Beat 1/3 cup of sugar until the

cream forms firm spikes. Add the whipped cream to the cooled marshmallow mixture.

4. Divide half of the cream mixture over the crust, place the peaches over the cream and divide the rest of the cream mixture over the peaches. Sprinkle the crumb mixture on the cream. Cool until ready to serve.

Macros

Per serving: 366 calories; 22.5 g of fat; 39.2 g carbohydrates; 1.9 g of protein; 68 mg of cholesterol; 190 mg of sodium

200. Blueberry Dessert

Prep time: 30 minutes
Servings: 28

Ingredients

- 1/2 cup butter
- 2 cups white sugar
- 36 graham crackers, crushed
- 4 eggs
- 2 packets of cream cheese, softened
- 1 teaspoon vanilla extract
- 2 cans of blueberry pie filling
- 1 package (16-oz) frozen whipped cream, thawed

Instructions

1. Melt the butter or margarine and add 1 cup of sugar and graham crackers. Squeeze this mixture into a 9x13 dish.
2. Beat the eggs. Gradually beat the cream cheese, sugar, and vanilla in the eggs.
3. Pour the mixture of eggs and cream cheese over the graham cracker crust. Bake for 15 to 20 minutes at 165 ° C (325 ° F). Cool.
4. Pour the blueberry pie filling on top of the baked dessert. Spread non-dairy whipped topping on fruit. Cool until ready to serve.

Macros

Per serving: 354 calories; 15.4 grams of fat; 50.9 g carbohydrates; 3.8 g of protein; 53 mg cholesterol; 199 mg of sodium

201. Frosty Strawberry Dessert

Prep time: 25 minutes
Servings: 16

Ingredients

- 1 cup flour
- 1/4 cup brown sugar
- 1/2 cup chopped walnuts
- 1/2 cup melted butter
- 1 cup of white sugar
- 2 cups of sliced strawberries
- 2 tablespoons lemon juice
- 1 cup whipped cream

Instructions

1. Bring the oven up to 175 ° C (350 ° F).
2. Mix the flour, brown sugar, nuts, and melted butter in a bowl. Spread on a baking sheet and bake for 20 minutes in the preheated oven until crispy. Remove from the oven and let cool completely.
3. Beat the egg whites to snow. Keep beating until you get firm spikes while slowly adding sugar. Mix the strawberries in the lemon juice and stir in the egg whites until the mixture turns slightly pink. Stir in the whipped cream until it is absorbed.
4. Crumble the walnut mixture and spread 2/3 evenly over the bottom of a 9-inch by 13-inch dish. Place the strawberry mixture on the crumbs and sprinkle the rest of the crumbs. Place in the freezer for two hours. Take them out of the freezer a few minutes before serving to facilitate cutting.

Macros

Per serving: 184 calories; 9.2 g fat; 24.6 g carbohydrates; 2.2 g of protein; 18 mg cholesterol; 54 mg of sodium.

202. Pumpkin Dessert

Prep time: 15 minutes
Servings: 16
Ingredients

- 1 (15-oz) can of pumpkin filling
- 12 ounces evaporated milk
- 1 cup of white sugar
- 3 eggs
- 4 teaspoons pumpkin pie herbs
- 1 (18-oz) package of yellow cake mix
- 3/4 cup of melted butter
- 1 1/2 cup chopped pecans

Instructions

1. Bring the oven up to 175 ° C (350 ° F). Grease a 9 x 13 inch baking dish.
2. Combine pumpkin, condensed milk, sugar, eggs and pumpkin pie in a bowl. Pour the pumpkin mixture into the prepared baking dish. Sprinkle the cake mixture over the pumpkin mixture; sprinkle with butter. Sprinkle the pecans over the layer of butter.
3. Bake in the preheated oven until the knife in the middle comes out clean, about 1 hour.

Macros

Per serving: 390 calories; 22.6 g fat; 44 g carbohydrates; 5.6 g of protein; 65 mg of cholesterol; 376 mg of sodium.

203. Mari's Dessert Pie

Prep time: 25 minutes
Servings: 12
Ingredients

- 1/2 cup butter
- 1 cup all-purpose flour
- 1/4 cup white sugar
- 1 package of cream cheese
- 1/2 cup of white sugar
- 8 oz whipped cream topping
- 1 (4-oz) package of instant chocolate pudding

Instructions

1. Bring the oven up to 175 ° C (350 ° F).
2. In a large bowl, mix butter, flour and 1/4 cup sugar until the mixture looks like coarse breadcrumbs. Push the mixture into the bottom of a 9 x 13-inch baking dish. Bake in the preheated oven for 15 to 18 minutes or until lightly browned to allow cooling to room temperature.
3. In a large bowl, beat cream cheese and 1/2 cup sugar until smooth. Stir in half of the whipped topping. Spread the mixture over the cooled crust.
4. Mix the pudding in the same bowl according to the instructions on the package. Spread over the cream cheese mixture.
5. Garnish with the remaining whipped cream. Cool in the fridge.

Macros

Per serving: 376 calories; 23 g fat; 39.9 g carbohydrates; 3.6 g of protein; 49 mg cholesterol; 294 mg of sodium

204. Baked Plum Pudding Dessert

Prep time: 10 minutes
Servings: 12

Ingredients

- 1/2 cup butter
- 3/4 cup white sugar
- 5 eggs
- 1 cup of dried currants
- 1 cup of golden raisins
- 1/2 cup of chopped pecans
- 1 tablespoon flour
- 3 cups of bread
- 2 teaspoons of ground cinnamon
- 1/2 teaspoon ground chili pepper
- 1/2 teaspoon ground clove
- 1/2 teaspoon pumpkin pie spice

Instructions

1. Bring the oven up to 175 ° C (350 ° F).
2. Cream butter and sugar together. Beat the eggs one by one until they are completely absorbed. Combine the currants, raisins, and pecans in a separate bowl with flour. Stir in the butter. Stir in bread, cinnamon, allspice, cloves, and pumpkin pie. Pour into an 8x8 inch baking dish.
3. Bake in the preheated oven for 40 minutes until the mixture is tender.

Macros

Per serving: 265 calories; 13.4 g of fat; 34.5 g carbohydrates; 4.6 g of protein; 98 mg of cholesterol; 146 mg of sodium.

Printed in the USA
CPSIA information can be obtained
at www.ICGtesting.com
LVHW082137080224
771392LV00005B/60